Public Relations Cases

for analysis and action

by John Ellerbach, Ed.D.

About the author: Ever since John Ellerbach was a St. Anthony friar (Go friars!) in Dubuque, Iowa, in the 60s, he has considered himself a creative communicator. In 8th grade, he did some awesome Oral English presentations. In high school, he wrote for the school newspaper. At the University of Dubuque, he read nearly every book in the library, wrote poetry and acted weird. Eventually, he became a news reporter and magazine writer. Then to Lima, Peru, for a stint as a teacher at Colegio Roosevelt. Next: to Drake for an M.A. and then off to the Iowa Hospital Association (IHA). He did PR for three years at IHA. He also wrote a couple of funny* books about Iowa. Then he earned a doctorate at Oklahoma State, followed by an academic gypsy lifestyle for 25 years, as he taught PR, advertising and journalism at seven different colleges and universities in the United States. So the dude has been around. He lives in the Smoky Mountains of North Carolina now and spends a lot of time editing the creative communications of his dear friend Dickie Fleegle. Ellerbach has two wonderful daughters, a devoted dog named Otis and a dedicated wife of 41 years, Andi, who copy edits and listens intently and still laughs when he tells her about all his dynamic Oral English presentations in The Eighth.

in his estimation

To purchase this book: It is available on Amazon.com, at CreateSpace.com and through DickieInTheEighth.com, where Ellerbach's good
friend sells it at a discount.

Preamble

Doesn't "Preamble" sound so much more scholarly than "Introduction"? Chuck Fleming would get a chuckle out of that.

Dr. Charles Fleming was my teacher, adviser and dissertation supervisor at Oklahoma State. That man was an inspiration. A retired Marine colonel, he came to OSU because he wanted to study mass communication higher education. He had already been a highly successful public relations practitioner. When I showed up in the late 80s, also very eager to learn about mass communication teaching, he was teaching graduate research classes and PR. I was most fortunate to have him as a professor.

Dr. Fleming was a patriot and a scholar. And he had a wonderful sense of humor. He particularly liked strange, silly names. I remember Petronious Sweetpits very well. Sweetpits sometimes made a cameo in Dr. Fleming's lectures and occasionally provided tidbits of wisdom in Dr. Fleming's handouts. Petronius was a wise (if somewhat silly) man.

This book is dedicated to the memory of Dr. Fleming. He died much too young. It is a shame that more master's and doctoral candidates at OSU did not get to know this exemplary educator. Yes, his standards were rigorous. Yet, he always knew how to throw an important bit of humor into the serious academic pursuit.

This book has fun with names. However, the cases are meant to be serious matter to challenge the brain matter: matter that really happened or really could happen. This book is based on an approach that Dr. Fleming taught me: relate your learning objectives to the not-too-distant needs of the students. So when I wrote *Public Relations Cases for Analysis and Action,* I did strive to make the content relevant and meaningful to the traditional PR student. You, the reader, ought to be able to vicariously participate in each of the 18 cases offered here. The questions and observations at the end of each case will help you analyze the situations. Then you should offer suggestions on how the characters in each case ought to proceed. If you have a PR professor even half as good as Dr. Fleming was, he or she will successfully lead you in the fascinating analysis process. Dr. Fleming led me in that direction many times. I'm simply paying it forward, colonel. Thanks for everything. (Oh, and if I ever get rich, I am going to give big bucks to OSU to establish the Fleming-Sweetpits-Jelloblock endowed **chair*** at OSU.

*or maybe at least a sturdy stool or a comfortable couch

Table of Contents:

What happens when a creative PR professor submits a play to your student-run drama group but his boss gets hold of the script and calls that creative work "dangerous"? Neah has just started the PR major, so she sure doesn't want to anger the head of the PR sequence. On the other hand, she also believes in free speech...

Case 1: A Double Major Leads to Double Jeopardy

Happy to Add a Second Major

You are Neah Phyte, 20. Your first two years at California Tech-Shasta (CTS) went by quickly. You entered as a theatre major and enjoyed the classes and working in various roles on productions, mostly behind the scenes. Now, as a junior, your work and dedication have earned you the right to be a key player in upcoming theatre projects. In fact, before the summer break, you were elected by your peers to the three-student governing board of the independent production company financed and run exclusively by students: Tech Talent. In the coming year, this ambitious group intends to stage three plays: two serious dramas and one comedy. The comedy script unanimously approved by your governing board is called *"Bernays: And We Ain't Talking the French Sauce!"* The script was written by a new CTS faculty member who teaches public relations, communication ethics and media law classes.

During the summer, when you work 40-hour weeks at Burger Barn, living at home and saving as much money as possible, your mother asks you if you intend to "study anything in college that might lead to a real job." She says, "I just can't stand the thought of such a bright young woman waiting tables the rest of her life, hoping to be 'discovered' as an actor. I'm not saying to drop your major," she tells you. "I'm just asking that you tack on another major 'to fall back on.'"

Mom does help with college expenses. Although she would never withhold funds because she doesn't approve of your major, you can tell that she wants to get the most from her investment in you—and you do feel a bit guilty that she might be right. Fortunately, you are able to offer good news: You intend to add a second major: public relations. PR is a growing field with good job prospects. "In fact," you tell her, "this fall I am going to do the PR for that comedy Tech Talent will produce in late October. And I'm very excited about not only being onstage as Bernays' activist wife, Doris, but also promoting the play. I intend to fill every seat in that auditorium for every performance."

Happy to Have a Ham

You feel very fortunate, as you had the foresight to take a PR Principles course during your fourth semester at Tech. Your drama professor recommended the professor, calling him a "ham at heart." You had not heard that slang before, but you soon learned by sitting in his classes that this PR guy, Dr. Lee Ivory, had no intention of reading from dog-eared lecture notes and displaying lifeless PowerPoints to define terms in the text. He was animated. Despite the fact that this was a lecture class of more than 60 students, he managed to be interactive. He wasn't content with standing in front of a crowd to lecture; he went into the crowd to ask questions and to seek out student reactions to the reading material. It was a fun class. Yes, he tended to "ham it up," but as encouragement for learning, not as entertainment only. In fact, PR Principles happened to be one of the most academically challenging courses you had had thus far. Your grade on the first exam led you to set up an appointment with the professor. OK, you were a bit miffed that you got an 84 percent. You are used to getting all As.

Lee Ivory is 39. At the time you took his intro course, he was just completing his first year at Tech. He has two young children and a wife who is a stay-at-home mom. Dr. Ivory had just completed a Ph.D. He seems very busy, but he also seems accessible to students. In fact, he has scheduled extra office hours to accommodate the 120 students and 50 advisees he has this semester. You get to see him right away.

"I really enjoy your teaching style," you tell him as you take a seat in his office.

"Cut the crap!" he blurts. Then he smiles and laughs heartily.

"Yep, that's the style!" you say.

"So you're here to tell me you like my style, or perhaps to question why you

Didn't get an 'A' on my first exam?

Wow, the guy is good, you think. Maybe you're not the first to see him about the exam grade.

The Ham Has a Script

Dr. Ivory takes out a copy of the exam and goes over each question with you. By the end of the session, you understand why you got that 84 percent instead of an "A." You are ready to leave when he says, "By the way, congratulations on being named to the Tech Talent board." You are impressed. Neah, you are one in 60 in the class, yet he knows something about you. "I wonder if you could do me a favor," he begins. And that's when your real-world education in public relations begins. He hands you a script and asks if your student board would read it as a possible offering for next year's Tech Talent productions. He notes that he has seen the posters from Tech Talent, asking for local writers to submit scripts.

"Of course, I don't know if I have talent…but I *am* local!" he quips. So you take the Bernays spoof back to your two other colleagues. All three of you do a table reading and love it. You immediately schedule Dr. Ivory's comedy for the first Tech Talent production in the upcoming fall, and you delight in knowing that you will be doing public relations for a play about public relations.

Bertie Gets Involved

You did get an "A" as the final grade in the PR Principles course, doing exceptionally well on the three other exams and the 20-page paper on "The Perception is the Reality" topic you chose. However, you soon learn that what you see as an innocent "spoof" is an entirely different reality for one of Dr. Ivory's colleagues and head of the PR sequence, Bernard "Bertie" Purr. Later, you will have a threatening memo to underscore just how different that "reality" really is.

Word of mouth is one of the best ways of creating buzz at Tech, a relatively small school of 5,000 students, most of them commuters. Over the summer, theatre majors and PR majors are already talking about what a great opening comedy Tech Talent has in store for fall. Professor Purr, 55, (M.A. in Curriculum Design from (CTS) has been with Tech for 15 years, having worked previously for 10 years as a PR director for the local hospital and then coming to Tech to start the PR undergraduate program there. He is very much in tune with the local grapevine. He knows that Dr. Ivory is popular with the students, and students have told Professor Purr how excited they are that a professor has written a comedy for them to produce. In fact, during the summer, Professor Purr comes for lunch at Burger Barn and you wait on him. Purr is friendly, but also tends to be "all business." He immediately asks if he can obtain a copy of the Ivory script. You smile and reply that you would be glad to get him one. "I can also sell you two tickets!" you say.

"I don't think that will be necessary," he replies. Purr gets the Burger Barn Big Wallop Meal to go. The next day, you drive to campus to drop the script off at his office.

Lee and Purr Have Harsh Words

Before you get to Professor Purr's door, you hear voices in the office and decide to wait outside until his open-door conference is finished. It soon becomes clear that he is talking to Dr. Ivory. You can overhear everything.

"Lee, I've made this PR arm of Communication into one of the best small school PR teaching initiatives in the country. Shucks, at least that's what the Shasta County PR chapter of PRSA folks tell me. Now what the heck am I going to tell them? They expect you to support their efforts. First, you are writing plays when you are supposed to be doing PR research. Second, you make fun of one of the founders of public relations. By the end of the first act, our PR program and our local PR practitioners are going to be the laughingstock of the county! I can't have that."

"It's just good fun, Professor Purr. Actually, I think we'll be perceived as a program that can laugh at itself, and I see that as positive. Maybe one of the best ways to show the absurdities of stereotypes is to exaggerate those absurdities. Besides, why don't you wait until you read the script before you come to such harsh conclusions?"

"Harsh conclusions? I've already heard so much student talk about "Fast Eddie" Bernays. It sounds like you've characterized him as a con man!" Then the door slams shut and Dr. Ivory leaves. He does not see you. You decide to leave the script in Professor Purr's faculty mailbox and go back home.

Lee Calls Neah

That night you get a call from Dr. Ivory. Actually, your mom answers the phone and starts up a conversation. She thanks Dr. Ivory for "being an inspiration" to her daughter. "I've never seen Neah so excited about a future job!" she says. When you get on the phone, Dr. Ivory makes jokes as usual, asking how his "favorite burger flipper for life" is doing. But then his tone gets serious. He reads an excerpt from a memo he has just received from the university's attorney. (See exhibit 1-A.) He tells you that all three Tech Talent leaders will be getting a copy of that memo soon. Then he offers the following:

A. "Neah, is it worth it to challenge this? I know your Tech Talent people consider yourselves proudly independent, much like the student newspaper staff does. You raise your own money and feel that free speech is essential. But this time, maybe you might consider dropping the spoof and doing a different play. Obviously, what is a spoof to some is an affront to others. Yeah, I know we encourage diversity— including the diversity of creativity and opinion on this campus— but maybe the PR satire is a bit too much of an outlier to be staged this year."

B. "I know that Professor Purr got a copy of the play from you. Funny, he could have asked me and I would have been glad to give it to him. He read it. He hates it. He feels threatened."

C. "I am only beginning my second year here. My thoughts are that maybe I'll wait to publish some creative writing until I get tenure. At this point, I think I might be able to patch things up with Powerful Purr. Yep, that's what they call him. (You interject that he is called "Gangbusters Bertie" and you both laugh.) Norm Dweebnubber is the titular department chair, but he never makes a move without consulting Professor Purr. It seems that Purr has strong allies in the provost's office."

For your consideration:

▶▶ 1-1: After you hang up the phone from talking to Dr. Ivory, what is the first step you would take to determine how to handle the situation?

▶▶ 1-2: Presuming that somewhere along the line you meet with your other two Tech Talent leaders, what are the major issues you three must discuss?

▶▶ 1-3: Note that the attorney's letter does not address the Tech Talent students directly, nor did anyone contact any one of your three leaders for comment and insight before the letter was sent.

▶▶ 1-4: Certainly you were looking forward to doing PR for the *"Bernays: And We Ain't Talking the French Sauce!"* production. If you do decide to go ahead with the production, in the light of these new circumstances, how will your initial public relations strategies regarding the play be changed—if they are changed at all? Would you go with the "they tried to censor us" angle to increase attendance?

▶▶ 1-5: It looks like Dr. Ivory has decided not to challenge the letter and perhaps will withdraw his play. You three Tech Talent leaders decide to meet with him. What happens in that meeting?

▶▶ 1-6: Does Professor Purr's intervention give you second thoughts about pursuing a second major in PR? Are all PR professors so protective of the image of their discipline? Are all professors in other departments the same way? Should they be?

➤➤ 1-7: It looks like a case of double jeopardy: You could damage your relationship with the head of the PR major and you could damage the reputation of Tech Talent. What to do?

Exhibit 1-A:

To: Dr. Leopold Ivory, Assistant Professor, Communications, CTS
From: Litta Gation, Counsel, California Technical at Shasta
Subject: Cease and desist
Date: August 10, 2016
Cc: Tech Talent Triumvirate: (Neah Phyte, Carlie Footlights, Will Spearshaker); Provost Ladderclimber, Dr. Dweebnubber and Professor Bernard Purr

It has come to my attention and the attention of the provost that you have supplied a script for use in the fall by our Tech Talent group, a drama club that puts on several plays each year. I and others have read your script, and we consider the material to be inappropriate for our students. In fact, we believe that the staging of such content will do irreparable damage to the reputation of our local public relations society as well as to our thriving PR program in the Communications Department. Therefore, we request that to avoid negative consequences regarding your pursuit of tenure and to ensure that our students are not corrupted by your insistence that they stage your play, you immediately withdraw that play from consideration as the first or as any play in Tech Talent's bill of fare. Be it known that this office has every intent of pursuing this matter to the fullest.

There is a time to challenge the system and a time to acquiesce in order to have the system validate you and your work. What time is it in this case? The student does consent to the separate internships, but now he is faced with what he believes is ongoing prejudice regarding his choice of a political candidate. Such prejudice could keep him from graduating with a PR major.

Case 2: A "Very Unique" Internship

Chad's Application Gets Reviewed

You are Chad Publicus, a 21-year-old student entering his senior year at Wisconsin Falls University, a private, nonsectarian school of 2,000 undergraduates located north of Milwaukee. You have completed all the requirements for your political science major (3.5/4.0 scale), and you only need the required capstone course and an internship to complete the requirements for your second major: public relations (so far: 3.2/4.0). Today the three-person Communication Arts Department faculty committee that approves internship proposals has scheduled a special meeting to take a closer look at your application. You are requested to attend. You ask if you may bring along your political science academic adviser. That request is granted.

Conducting the meeting is Cronkite "Cranky" Elmer-Davis, professor of Communication Arts and head of the journalism sequence. Elmer-Davis came to WFU eight years ago, taking early retirement from a position as editor of the editorial page at the *Milwaukee Journal-Sentinel*. He likes to make meetings swift and productive. Therefore, as soon as all five meeting participants are assembled, he clears his throat: "We all know everybody here, more or less, so let's get started…" Then he begins reading from your internship proposal:

This summer internship experience will prove to be a very unique experience… he reads. All four professors at the table have been provided copies of your application.

"Uh, Mr. Publicus, I know you have been exposed to this in my classes, but just to remind you: unique words like 'unique' cannot be qualified. A slip-up, no doubt, acceptable to the very flexible Political Science Department, but not acceptable to Communication Arts."

You grin sheepishly and wait for your political science mentor, E. Lector Ballot, 44, to smile and offer one of his characteristically snappy comebacks. Instead, a scowl and eyes averted. The rumors must be true: these two departments hate each other. Professor Elmer-Davis continues reading:

My big concern is the time commitment. Its all summer, at least 300 clock hours, twice the required hours for three credits in the required Com Arts internship. So I request that this internship be co-sponsored by Political Science so I can also get three credits from them.

"Do note, folks, that Mr. Publicus is still struggling with discerning the difference between the two forms of 'its.' Do note that," says Elmer-Davis.

Does the Student Fully Understand the Nature of the Internship?

So far, Professor Ballot has said nothing. Sitting next to him is the head of the public relations sequence, Carla Query, 28. She is a Wisconsin Falls summa cum laude philosophy graduate who holds an M.S. from UW-Milwaukee in public relations and a Ph.D. from Wisconsin Madison in interpersonal communication theory. She has spent all of her adult life in school and has no professional PR background. "May I ask Mr. Publicus if he fully understands the nature of his internship duties?" says Dr. Query. This is where Professor Ballot chimes in:

"We have discussed the candidate at length," Ballot says.

"And ad nauseum, I presume," interjects the third member of the committee, Tyler Tiebow, 61, half-time senior adjunct who teaches two sections of the PR capstone course every spring. This is Tiebow's second year at the Falls. He worked as a marketing specialist for General Motors for more than 20 years. It also becomes very clear to you that Tiebow, whom you will have next spring for capstone, hates the political candidate you want to work for. "I'm just concerned that an impressionable student like Mr. Publicus would be forever jaundiced by the political process by doing an internship for David Petty. I've got several internships I could hook this student up with that would be more suitable to his public relations education and much more beneficial for his future in PR. How a political candidate can hold a gun to the head of big industry and demand they not take advantage of better labor deals elsewhere is an outrage. We don't need our students involved with that kind of garbage."

Ballot: "But are you really concerned for his education, or actually concerned that a pioneer like David Petty is disproving some of your sacred principles of public relations? One of which is: Always suck up to the media." This time Ballot does not avert his eyes, but looks straight into Tiebow's.

Dr. Query attempts to break the tension: "Well, on one hand I know we cannot shelter our students from reality. But on the other hand, David Petty does have some rather disturbing idiosyncrasies."

"Like he hates the media and berates them in public," adds Elmer-Davis. "Since the media provide him all that free coverage, such crass behavior seems…seems uncalled for and very unsettling. But let me read more from this young man's internship application…"

More is Read from the Application

David Petty is my idle. We need him as our Wisconsin senator. I want to use my public relations skills and political science knowledge to help ensure that he represent those of us who believe America is being taken over by outside interests, some subversive and some internal, like industry that will take away our jobs.

Says Elmer-Davis: "And let me make more than an idle comment here. I am not comfortable allowing our student to be smothered under the tutelage of a demagogue, even though I hear the interns never meet the guy, as they are too busy stuffing envelopes, making phone calls and carrying signs that say, 'Gun

14

'Unholstered, Petty Will Protect us from Interlopers!' And I don't think that's clever and I doubt I need to read any more of this application to immediately request of this committee that said application be turned down and that senior adjunct Tiebow use his impressive list of contacts to find a more suitable internship for our student."

Two Internships

Chad did not want the internship the Communication Arts Department found for him: 150 clock hours working for the Milwaukee Housing Authority (MHA). But it came down to this: Either take PR as a minor (no required internship) or go to the MHA and, according to Professor Ballot, "paint houses." Your political science mentor advised you to do two internships. His department would sponsor and supervise your Petty experience.

As it turned out, the MHA experience did involve more than a brush and a roller. In fact, your on-site supervisor was quite attentive to your needs and provided experiences in the writing of news releases and involvement in several special events. On the other hand, the Petty internship did not provide consistent supervision and guidance. However, Petty's campaign manager did meet once with Chad briefly and advised him to keep a journal: "Since PR is your major, write down everything our candidate does that goes against the traditional wisdom—because it isn't wisdom at all. The old, tired ways of public relations desperately need to be challenged and new ways need to emerge." Those copious journal entries would later be the basis of your capstone mini-thesis paper in Professor Tiebow's PR Issues course. You got a "D-" on that paper.

The Paper

Since the paper comprised half the grade in the Issues class, you were in trouble that spring. You could still graduate, but you could not claim the PR major, as Issues had to be completed with a grade of "C" or better. (The other half of the grade consisted of class participation. While you were vocally active throughout the semester, it was clear to you that Professor Tiebow tried to ignore you and your comments when possible. In fact, one time you and he got into a "heated" discussion over whether PRSA and their certification credential, APR, was essential to the reputation of the industry and the professional growth of the PR practitioner. You took the stance that the organization and its credential was a manipulation to make all people who did PR "fall in line like so many sheep." You urged that your fellow students would better serve their careers and the PR industry by being independent and eschewing the APR designation.)

Chad was so fascinated by the notion that PR is "of the people" and not a "bureaucratic leash holding back the best, honest efforts of practitioners," (quotes from his notes) that his 30-page capstone mini-thesis focused on that populist and leash topic that he began mulling over during the summer. To make certain his paper was a good one, Chad asked Dr. Ballot to read it and offer suggestions. He did. He had Chad change the title. The Original title: "PR Accreditation is a Bastardization of Free Speech." He changed it to: "Is Accreditation Right for Every Public Relations Practitioner? A Discussion of Alternatives to the APR Credential." Evidently, Chad, the toned down title and what you thought was "balanced" content still angered Professor Tiebow. He gave it a 61 percent. And he gave you a 78 percent for class participation. Final grade: 69 percent. D+.

The Grade Challenge

Capstone, two sections, was offered only every spring. Your first request was that Communication Arts offer it as an independent study in the coming summer. Therefore, you could take it again, pass it and get your PR major as part of the degree. The department turned that down. So your next move was to go through the grade challenge process. You claimed that Professor Tiebow had no real quantitative measure for performance on either the paper or participation. After you filed your grade challenge, the department head gave copies of your paper to all Communication Arts members to grade: The grades came back as follows: 51 percent, 53 percent, 59 percent, 60 percent and 61 percent. In addition, since four of the five faculty members had had you in class, they were also asked, as best they could remember, to grade your participation: 70 percent, 75 percent and 78 percent. Therefore, the department determined that your grade challenge had no significant merit.

For your consideration:

➵ 2-1: Should you continue the grade-challenge process? You suspect that the department was simply covering for a colleague. But can you prove it? The next step: taking your case to the Dean of the College.

➵ 2-2: If you truly believe that an effective PR practitioner must be free from too much, as candidate (and now senator) Petty put it, "brainwashing by the power elite," why even fight to get the PR major as part of your degree? After all, the practice of PR requires nothing in terms of education or credentials. You can still do PR regardless of your degree.

➵ 2-3: You yearn to begin your career as a political public relations specialist. Obviously, it would not be wise to use any of your Communications Arts faculty members as references. But how candid should you be when interviewing for PR jobs regarding the fact that a PR "minor" was the result of your PR education?

➵ 2-4: What about making your case with the student-run media? Should your grade challenge become a public relations case study in and of itself? What is the downside of doing so? By being a Petty supporter on a decidedly liberal campus, is your credibility compromised?

A happy secretary a happy department makes. You have often heard this. But how far do you go before you cannot overlook certain unprofessional behavior that seems to delight the secretary? You have been told time and again that in your future PR job, if the secretary likes you, life will be so much easier. This one is not going to like you very much if you blow the whistle on her. And neither is her boss.

Case 3: Secretarial Recommendation Dilemma: Given the Circumstances, What to Do?

You Overheard Plenty

You, Donna Pleasant, 25, are sitting on a chair in the departmental office, waiting for your appointment with your academic adviser and Journalism/PR Department head Dolores Fleishperson. While you wait (her door is closed), department secretary Conchetta Sanchez answers the phone, and you hear the following:

"Dr. Dolores is in conference and not available. If you tell me what this is about, perhaps I can help….I see. Well, simply give me the name of the student and I can provide the necessary background. As an assistant administrator, I know these students very well, sometimes even better than Dr. Dolores herself."

You infer that the caller is asking for a job reference, and you wait for Conchetta to say goodbye and hang up, noting that certainly the person on the other end is a professional and would certainly not substitute the secretary's remarks for Dr. Fleishperson's impending insights. But the conversation goes on…

"Ernie Stonefeld? You got his application? Stony? Yes, he graduated in the spring. Vice president of our PRSSA chapter last semester. I've known him all five years he was here. He took some extra time to get that grade average up there and cut down on the beer. I'd say he might be able to handle your Web site and do some adequate video work, although I can help you out by giving you the names of a couple of stronger recent graduates who would do much better, if you care to contact them…"

What? What did you just hear? So the rumors you thought were lies are actually true. Conchetta does overstep her bounds and do work solely intended for the chair. And she does it out in the open, with no regard for privacy. This scenario so much upsets you that you immediately leave the office, walk outside and dial Dr. Fleishperson's direct line. Instead, it goes to Conchetta's phone, and she answers. There is an awkward silence. Then, "Uh, Conchetta, this is Donna Pleasant. I was sitting waiting for Dr. Fleishperson, but I suddenly do not feel well, so I'm walking back to my apartment. I wanted to leave a voice mail to tell her I'll need to reschedule my advising appointment."

"Her voice mail is not accessible now, Donna. But I'll tell her. I pretty much keep track of everything around here involving Dr. D anyway…"

The truth: You had hoped to leave a message on her voice-mail to alert Dr. Dolores to the conversation you had just witnessed and to ask her to meet you outside. In the past, students claimed that Conchetta often listened in on Dr. Fleishperson's office conversations. You aren't sure how, but you do know the wall is thin and that her desk is next to the wall.

"Besides, honey, I check her voice mail for her regularly…"

"Honey" Chosen to Represent Many

OK, maybe you were one of the last holdouts of the majority of the majors who do not trust Conchetta. At 25, at least three years older than most of your cohorts, you consider yourself a bit more experienced when it comes to assessing others' character. Before becoming a PR major at Burgh Haven University of Pennsylvania, you spent three years as a secretary yourself in a busy office environment. You know that sometimes secretaries are taken for granted by bosses and can be innocent victims of nasty rumors. Therefore, you always gave Conchetta the benefit of the doubt when other students would complain about her brusqueness, her power grabs, her meddlesomeness, her overstepping authority and her blatant favoritism when it came to students. But no more benefit and no more doubt. A day goes by and you are still upset. By that time, you have contacted

19

several student leaders in your major. They all ask you to do the same thing: Enlighten Dr. Fleishperson. Immediately. Tell her you represent many of her majors who have seen and heard dozens of disturbing things regarding Conchetta's lack of professionalism. Tell the department head this behavior has got to stop. They all also point out that you are likely one of Fleishperson's favorites. You have yet to fully acknowledge this to yourself, but you do know she sees you as a mature, serious, hard-working student. So you reschedule the appointment.

It's Your Fault for Overhearing?

Dr. Dolores Fleishperson listens attentively. When you relate what you overheard the other day and then tell her about several other students' embarrassing experiences with Conchetta, she nods and waits until you have finished. Then she says something that surprises you: "Donna, as soon as you heard that this was a recommendation call, you should have stepped outside the office and not listened in."

What?

We all Have Our Blind Spots

You cannot believe that Dr. D would possibly blame you for violating privacy in a common departmental area where people come and go all the time. Furthermore, she adds this: "Conchetta has been my devoted eyes and ears for the past five years, ever since I took on this crazy department head job. She's underpaid but darn near indispensable. Besides, perhaps what you overheard isn't exactly the way things were. Although, doggone it, I have never known Conchetta to be wrong about any student. Ever. It sounds to me like she was trying to be as helpful as possible to a prospective employer. You have to appreciate that."

What? Sure, you know from experience that we all have differing perceptions regarding other people. But could Dr. Fleishperson be completely blind to the truth about her secretary?

The Real Zinger

Conchetta does often act in a condescending manner to a number of faculty members, even when students are within earshot. It is clear that at least three of the seven faculty members in the department go out of their way to avoid her. One faculty member confided to you that "Dr. D will defend her to the bitter end. Conchetta could kill D's husband with a letter opener right in front of her eyes and she'd somehow tell other eyewitnesses, "Well, you have to appreciate that.""

Then the zinger from Dr. D before you left her office: "I know this semester is your last, Donna. Perhaps it might be best that you not use me as a reference, given the current circumstances. Besides, I am now wondering about your attitude toward protected classes. Conchetta is in a protected class, you know."

For your consideration:

➡ 3-1: Did Conchetta refer to herself on the phone as an "assistant administrator" or an "administrative assistant"? If the former, isn't she misrepresenting herself? If this is the case, should you take this and other complaints "over the head" of Dr. Fleishperson to the dean? Or maybe go to Human Resources?

➡ 3-2: OK, there are rumors that Conchetta and Dr. Fleishperson are having an affair. That one you refuse to believe. Never has any evidence been forthcoming to verify that. Just because you want to believe the worst does not mean the worst exists. Besides, as a former secretary, you do observe that Conchetta tends to get a lot of work done and, by and large, keep the department running smoothly. She definitely has her good qualities.

➡ 3-3: It seems that many people who should have some influence in the matter have given up and accept Conchetta for what she does and for how she is protected by Dr. Fleishperson—and how Conchetta protects her boss. Maybe the best way to get along is to go along? We all have shortcomings, right? You have no clout in the department. Your biggest need is to graduate summa cum laude and "graduate" from secretary to public relations assistant. If the Conchetta matter gets in the way, that could be devastating to your future career, right? Internal departmental PR matters are not your concern, right? You are almost out of there. Gut it out and stay out of trouble? But what if what happened to Stony could happen to you? What if prospective employers call the department and Conchetta says nasty things about *you*?

➤➤ 3-4: And this business about "protected class"? You consider yourself a champion of those who may have been discriminated against in the past. You carefully consider what Dr. Fleishperson said to you about "protected class." Your conclusion: Dr. Fleishperson has insulted you. You firmly believe it is wrong to protect anyone who behaves unethically, regardless of ethnicity.

➤➤ 3-5: One more thing: Another faculty member has opened up to you off the record. He says, "Don't bother. Even if Conchetta could be replaced, who's to say we wouldn't end up with somebody worse who transfers in? We'll just get another department's set of problems. I've heard plenty of horror stories from other departments here at Burgh Haven. Better the secretary devil you know than one you don't."

You are honored to be the first student at your university to serve on a search committee to hire a faculty member. Wow, will that look great on the resume! But what exactly do they allow you to do? Shouldn't you be doing more? And shouldn't you, as a student journalist, feel free to write about the experience? However, the dean wants to see and edit your broadcast story (if you decide to do one) ahead of time, noting that the hiring process "should not be compromised by an insider who has a major conflict of interest."

Case 4: A Student Journalist's Inside Look at the Faculty Hiring Process

Your University Touts Itself as Progressive

Your photo—yes, *your photo* appears on page 1 of the weekly, award-winning student newspaper (print and online editions) *Gopherland Goingson*! The cutline: *Gray Gopher senior Charlie Tunis (LA-PR and PJ) is all smiles as he stands between Mass Communication Department head Dr. Knockle Hedd and Liberal Arts Dean Ima Real-Pedante. Tunis is the first Gray Gopher student ever selected to serve on a committee to recruit and hire a faculty member. The Mass Communication Department is searching for a PR professor.*

The accompanying story quotes Dr. Hedd: "Minnesota Southeastern (North Campus) has always been a progressive institution. We believe we are on the cutting edge of the immersion of our students into as much real life as they can handle. We're proud to include Mr. Tunis, whose background includes a double emphasis in PR and broadcast journalism, as a non-voting member of the search committee to choose our next outstanding public relations faculty member. We look forward to his candid input at appropriate times in the all-important search process."

Your mom already has the photo and story posted on her refrigerator. Your peers in the Comm major give you all kinds of advice, including the following:

A. "Don't let them pick somebody dull. Before he left for the Ivy League, Doc Barnum was a real snoozer. And we could never find him in his office. Get somebody who shows up. And who has a pulse."

B. "Get somebody who has worked in the public relations field. Doc Emanuelle Kant is a sweet woman and a real easy grader. And she got a "SUPER HOT!"— THREE red chili peppers— rating on "Assess Your Profs Online." But we really don't learn squat, especially when she lectures so much about her doctoral dissertation on persuasion habits and rituals in small groups of monkeys. I'm afraid I won't be ready for the next PR courses in the sequence. Hell, nobody I know even bought the Intro textbook last semester—and we all got As!"

C. "So you got three Comm profs and one so-called "outsider" prof from Marketing and you on that committee. Don't let 'em bully you, Chuck. Heck, you ain't the intimidated kind, but I'm just saying not to let them do anything stupid."

Anything *Stupid?* These are PROFESSIONALS!

Here is the quote the newspaper used from you: "I am honored to be chosen as the student voice in a process I deeply respect. It is a rigorous selection process that has endured for many decades, and I am in awe of the defined procedures and meticulous scrutiny I will be a part of. I won't let the students I represent down and I will do the school I so much respect proud. Southeastern deserves the best faculty members, and we intend to find another." (Your mom highlighted the quote in fluorescent yellow on her fridge copy of the story.)

Stupid? You truly believe in the quote you gave to the newspaper. So as soon as the advertisement for the position is published online at Facultyjobs.com and online and in print in the *Chronicle of Higher Education*, you read it over and over again. (See appendix 4-A for the ad copy.) You note that the deadline for receipt of applications is exactly 12 weeks from the time of publication of the ad, published December 15. This means that committee work should get into high gear by mid-March. In the meantime, since review of applications will be "ongoing," you do expect you will receive and review all documentation as it comes in. "That only makes sense," you tell yourself. "That way, we keep up with the flow and don't get bogged down with a big stack of resumes on March 16." However, during the required one-hour search procedures orientation for the committee, given by a representative from Human Resources and by the school's affirmative action/equal opportunity director, you learn otherwise. You take notes. Here are the highlights of your notes:

A. Yes, screening ongoing, but not by committee. Only HR and AA/EO personnel to "identify protected classes and those with special consideration."

B. All application materials electronically submitted; but when committee gets info on March 16, paper copies only—and not to be duplicated. Paper copies folder of applicant materials locked in safe at HR. Committee members given two-hour stints in special room to review all documents. May return for two-hour stints as necessary.

C. HR will not provide committee with applications that are not complete by deadline.

D. Committee to draft quantitative (numbers assessment) evaluation document to be filled out for each candidate. Ex: Assign 10 points for terminal degree, up to 10 for significant teaching experience, etc.

E. Received "more than 1,000" applications for a history opening last year. Some fields lots of apps. Others, not.

F. When all committee eval docs completed, HR to tally scores and provide average scores for all candidates from all committee members. Duh! Ask if I get to look over the folders and do the eval document. Damn! HR guy says that isn't in the protocol, as I am an "observer" and "adviser" only. Double damn! How can I advise if I know nothing about the candidates? See Dr. Hedd and Real-Pedante about this!!! That's stupid! See Hedd!

"Good PR" but You Don't Get to Score

Hedd: "What does the dean say? She knows protocol. Call her for the determination, Chuck."

Real-Pedante: "Charles, it's good PR for the university and your department to have a student on the committee, but it is my determination that you are a participant-observer only. So you won't be in on the scoring. Sorry I missed your phone call. I hope voice mail is sufficient to clarify matters."

My Notes? My Notes!

Hedd: "Dr. Hedd here. *(voice mail)* How's that Valentine's special coming along on Gopher Vision? Looking forward to it. That live weekly news program has made great strides since you took over last December, Chuck. Good work. Oh, and by the way, HR wants you to turn in the notes you took at the committee orientation. Everything is supposed to be kept in a file, including all notes. Thanks! Sorry you missed my call. And, hey, don't forget that the missus and I were married on Valentine's Day. Happy to do an interview for your special!"

Ouch. Your notes with two naughty "d" words in them are now on the record. Will they think you have a negative attitude?

Gopher Vision Leaders Meet

What Dr. Hedd has said are "the best four Gopher Vision managers we have ever had" meet at the request of their president: you. You explain how disappointed you are in your role in the process.

"What that means is we cannot do a story on the process itself," says your V.P. of production, Danica Pondlilly. "That would be wrong. You have an axe to grind. Let's just stick to the Valentine's packages and wait to see what happens next with your faculty search assignment. Maybe they'll gradually let you in on more of the process. Give them some time."

"Agreed," says Howard Sturm, news anchor. "I've got a shot at a reporter job in Joplin, Missouri. I sure don't want them finding out that now we're doing investigative reporting and pissing off the administration by using confidential, insider information from employment searches. I need that stellar, unblemished recommendation from Hedd. And, yeah, great idea to interview him for one of the Valentine's packages. Also talk to that three-pepper hottie who teaches PR. She's single. And she'll provide some great photogenic stuff!"

Another colleague, ad sequence student Olga Davidvy adds: "Too early to criticize and panic, Chuck. Let it all play out. If you want, however, we can do a piece on how grateful you are to be part of the process and, of course, we can describe the process thus far, as long as we run the story past HR and AA/EO to make sure we aren't violating any labor or hiring laws."

Maybe it's just your level of frustration now, but you have never been more disappointed in a group of student colleagues in all your life. "Have they forgotten that they are journalists first and suck-ups second?" you ask your girlfriend. "Whatever happened to the fourth estate as watchdog?"

Some Good News

The dean has determined that you may have your two-hour stints in the HR room to look at the stacks of applications. She cautions you not to say anything about your perusals to anyone, including committee members outside of official search committee meetings, the first of which has been postponed from April 1 to April 10 because two of the committee members have yet to do an initial review of the applications and because AA/EO has requested more time to scrutinize applications.

This development has given you some hope and a modicum of trust in the process. It is well-known among students that a favorite professor who left three years ago to pursue a Ph.D. is applying for the job. You are eager to see his credentials and read what is sure to be an insightful, creative cover letter. You have no doubt this outstanding professor will be one of the top three candidates invited for an interview.

Two Hours in Isolation

A lengthy memo signed by the HR and AA/EO people assigned to this search is attached to each of 16 folders. Only sixteen? Well, Dr. Hedd did note that PR faculty jobs, particularly those that require the Ph.D., practical experience and significant teaching experience "do not yield 1,000 applications like a history opening would." Hedd tells you: "We're way out here in the Minnesota sticks, so we have to compete with the big city schools that offer better salaries and a lighter workload. By the way, whenever the ad touts 'excellent benefits,' that means the salary is crap. And the candidate has got to drive 85 miles an hour to make it to the Mini Apple suburbs in an hour. Who wants to drive that in winter?" But only sixteen? The memo explains that 22 applications were received by deadline. Six were discarded because they did not contain all seven required elements: three letters of recommendation, vita, cover letter, teaching philosophy, copies of student evaluations, copies of transcripts and evidence of scholarly work. You immediately note that the former professor's materials are in the stack of 16. You soon discover, however, that five of the 16 applicants do not meet the minimum standards to qualify for the job. That leaves 11 applications for you to review. However, no quantitative form is provided for you (memo says that "student observer/adviser has no vote and therefore has no required quantitative input"). Still, it is very clear to you that Professor Former is easily the number-one candidate. That should be clear to anyone. By far. No question in your mind.

The Tabulations are Finally in!

The committee convenes immediately after spring break. They have before them the names of the top three candidates who will be invited for interviews. That list does not include Professor Former. You wait and listen to discussion, holding the question about Former until the end of the session. Committee chair (and your favorite professor) Dr. Geisel Sues tells the group that HR and AA/EO has "moved up" three candidates: one has been identified as a military veteran, one as handicapped and one as a protected minority. They will all be called in for interviews ASAP. It is a short meeting. You decide to wait on your question about Dr. Former.

They Get Snapped Up Fast!

The next day, Dr. Sues emails committee members that all three candidates have been contacted, but all three already have job commitments for the fall. He tells the committee he will request that we "dip back into the pool" to come up with three more candidates to bring to campus. He reminds the committee that good PR professors get good jobs quickly. Having carefully gone over each candidate folder, you wonder if any of those three could even be classified as "good," and you are secretly glad that, in your estimation, at least two very strong candidates remain in that pool, including Dr. Former.

The Dead Pool

A week goes by. It is getting close to finals time. Finally, the committee, with carbon copies to Dr. Hedd, the provost, HR and AA/EO, gets a memo from the dean. The document says that she has "no choice but to cancel the search." She goes on to say that "the pool was shallow to begin with" and "now that we have lost our top people, we will wait until fall and re-advertise...In the meantime, we will employ extra adjuncts to fill the position."

For your consideration:

▶▶ 4-1: Dr. Hedd tells Dr. Sues who eventually tells you that "in March, I felt very uncomfortable taking a phone call from Dr. Former. He wanted to know how the search was coming along, and he said he missed the students at Minnesota Southeastern (North Campus). Hedd said he did report the phone call to HR, as required. It is clear that like you, Sues favored Former. As a committee member, is it worth it for you to pursue questioning on this matter?

▶▶ 4-2: Is now the time (last live broadcast of the season coming up next week) for you to do a story on your experience with the search? The newspaper is preparing its final edition, and the editor tells you she already has plenty of quotes from Dr. Hedd and Dr. Sues, both of whom lament the search failure but praise the process. Both also say "some very nice things" about you as the first student to serve on a faculty search committee. How does that make you feel?

➡ 4-3: You get a note from the head of HR. She thanks you for your committee service and reminds you that "all facets of the search process must remain confidential." How should you reply to that? (She sends a cc to Dr. Hedd, and Hedd sends you an email. He tells you he wants to see and edit your piece on the search process, should you decide to do one. But he recommends that you don't do one. "Clear conflict of interest," he notes.)

➡ 4-4: A faculty member in the Speech Department tells you off the record that "The best people seldom get hired, particularly at Goofy U (his slang for 'Gopher.') The system is so slow it stinks. Somebody ought to have the guts to overhaul this mess. Sure, the process is full of 'protections.' It's a real protection racket. Oh, and don't count on me to lead that charge for reformation. I'm up for tenure next year. So if you do a story, what I just told you is off the record."

➡ 4-5: Should you ask to see the quantitative "report cards" that each committee member filled out? (see appendix 4-B) Is it your right as a journalist? You are astounded that Professor Former was not at the top in terms of total points.

Exhibit 4-A: Text of the advertisement

The Department of Mass Communication at Minnesota Southeastern (North Campus) invites applications for a full-time, tenure track assistant professor of public relations to begin in August.

Minnesota Southeastern (North Campus) is located just an hour south of cosmopolitan Minneapolis on the majestic Mississippi River. MSNC is nationally recognized as a "best buy" institution for students (*Campus News Magazine*) and has an international reputation as a leader in Partnerships for Peace, an organization that promotes courses in peace studies throughout the world. The MSNC Department of Mass Communication takes great pride in fostering a spirit of independence in its students, helping them to become fair and objective communicators who use research to support their thoroughgoing efforts. We believe that no matter which of our four sequences the student chooses (PR, advertising, electronic media/broadcasting or print journalism) that the student should be afforded as much latitude as possible under the First Amendment.

The selected candidate would be expected to teach courses that support our curriculum, including but not limited to: Peace Studies Public Relations, Advertising Principles, Healthcare Public Relations, Digital/Social Media, Digital Media Production, Crisis Communications and Media Law/Ethics. All faculty members in the department are also expected to teach core courses, including Public Speaking. The ideal candidate's skill set will include experience with nonprofit organizations, corporate communication and strategic communication research. An active research agenda or the potential for top-level scholarship in the PR field is required. Proficiency with Adobe Creative Suite is highly valued. Use of and expertise regarding social media is expected. The teaching load is 4:4, with opportunities for summer teaching, if available. In addition, the successful candidate will be responsible for supporting our recruiting efforts and our student organizations, including the advising of a very active PRSSA chapter.

Salary is competitive with comparable schools and we have excellent benefits. A Ph.D. in public relations, mass communication or a closely related field is required and must have been completed before the August start. At least two years' successful teaching at the university level is also required for this position.

Review of applications will begin immediately, with the deadline for receipt of all applications March 15. No partial applications will be considered. Please send via one electronic file (Go to the *GrayGopherHR.com* site for complete application instructions) the following materials: cover letter, vitae, three recent letters of recommendation, evidence of scholarship, student evaluations summaries, one page philosophy of teaching and copies of unofficial transcripts. Minnesota Southeastern (North Campus) is devoted to diversity. We are an Affirmative Action/Equal Opportunity Employer, and we heartily welcome applications from protected classes. A successful criminal background check will be required as a condition of employment. Please direct all inquiries to zeldap@senchr.edu.

Exhibit 4-B:

Position #666912: MC-PR Assistant: Official Quantitative Assessment Tool for the Committee. (Approved by HR and AA/EO.)

1.____(10 points maximum)
Doctorate in MC/PR or closely related field? Please include in your quantification (0—10) strength of education as manifested in transcripts.

2.____(10 points maximum)
At least TWO years' successful university teaching experience. Please consider the courses taught as they relate to our needs. Also take into account student evaluations. Does the candidate have any background in the advising of student organizations? Does the candidate's philosophy of teaching meld with our university and departmental missions?

3.____(10 points maximum)
Professional experience in nonprofit, corporate and/or strategic research.

4.____(10 points maximum)
Evidence of or potential for meaningful scholarship.

5.____(5 points maximum)
Other skills: social media, Adobe Creative Suite, etc.

6.___(10 points maximum) **FOR HR AND AA/EO personnel to determine and assess)**
Do we have strong indications of this candidate's background regarding our promotion of diversity and our devotion to the protection of certain underrepresented or historically disadvantaged groups? (This includes military service background.) Committee members are to leave this (#5) blank. *For HR and AA/EO use only.*

Total_____/55   **Name of applicant:_____**

Today's date: _____   Signature of evaluator:_____

Case 5: Thank You for not Fuming (or Exploding)

"Smoking" is a Fun Book to Read

You are Shawna Polyglot. You love languages. You grew up in a bi-lingual household (English and Japanese), studied French throughout elementary school and spent a year in Peru as a high school exchange student. You have a triple major: Spanish, public relations and English. You attend Indiana Tech. You hope to someday return to Peru as a PR representative for an American-based fundraising organization to address poverty in Peru and, eventually, when you get a few years behind you, write about your experiences. This semester, you are taking a Recent American Fiction course with the renowned F. "Scotty" Gerald Fitzway, and you love it. Despite Tech having 30,000 students, it still does offer some small courses. This course is a seminar limited to 13 students, a seminar each student had to apply for with a written essay. Halfway through the semester, your class is now reading *Thank You for Smoking* by Christopher Buckley. You are having fun reading it.

Professor Fitzway: I presume because you are all English majors that you have a healthy disdain for public relations, right?

You: *(raising your hand)* Well, actually, another one of my majors is public relations.

Fitzway: I see. Nothing wrong with that, I guess. Of course, I would be very interested in your take on the ethics—or lack thereof—of Nick Naylor.

You: He's a sleazebag.

Student A: What? He's practicing the profession that you want to enter!

Student B: And he's representing a product that kills people.

You: True. But I don't want to be anything like he is. And I don't believe that Nick is really representative of the average PR practitioner. No way.

Fitzway: But you do want to do PR. Is it the money?

You: No. But I firmly believe that all issues and organizations ought to have access to those who understand and perform roles of advocacy. And I further believe that PR skills can do good for communities, especially if one works for the nonprofits.

Fitzway: So you do believe everyone—even the sleazebags—should be entitled to a professional communicator. Kind of like an attorney in a court of law.

You: Kind of like that.

Then it happens. There always seems to be one in every class: the blustery one: the one who gets all "inspired" by his own opinions and lets loose.

Brusque N. Blustery: I cannot believe somebody as seemingly talented as you are Shawna, is going to cheapen herself by being a spin doctor. Are we not supposed to learn from literature? I would think that after Buckley published *"Thank You"* that thousands of PR majors would have switched to other majors— majors they could live with, majors that would not keep them up nights with guilty consciences.

You: Like political science?

Blustery: There are some decent politicians out there.

You: Just as there are some decent PR practitioners. Most, in fact. As I said, I like the ones who work for nonprofits.

Blustery: Maybe they're decent at first, but they all eventually succumb to lying for their clients. You can't get ahead unless you do. And nonprofits don't tend to pay squat. I give you a few years and you'll go over to the for-profit side.

Fitzway: I have to admit I'm anti-PR.

You: Will that affect my grade? *(everyone laughs)* Is there anything I can do or say that will convince you and Blustery that PR is important to society? And, by the way, after Buckley's book came out, PR enrollments in universities continued to go up. In fact, even today the outlook for the future looks really great for PR majors.

Fitzway: My main objection is that these folks are not really educated. They know little about liberal learning. Most just want to memorize the rules to be successful, big-dollar earning hacks. And I don't think anybody will ever change my mind about that. In fact, the best schools in this nation do not even offer a PR degree. Anybody well-educated can go into PR if they want to; they don't need any special training. Advertising is the same way. You know what they say: The sound of selling is the dirge of our times.

Blustery: *(He's fuming now).* I will never change my mind, either! The more we legitimize lying in our universities and in our businesses, the worse the nation becomes!

You: …

For your consideration:

➤ 5-1: Fill in the space after the ellipsis with your response to Blustery, if any response.

➤ 5-2: One of the principles of PR is that it is largely a waste of time and resources to address and try to convert anyone zealously opposed to your cause. Do you really want to continue the "discussion" in this class with Blustery and others?

➤ 5-3: At the end of the class, the professor takes you aside and thanks you for "not exploding" when several students, including Blustery, viciously attack your chosen major and likely profession. He claims he, himself, was just playing devil's advocate. What do you say to him?

▶▶ 5-4: Professor Fitzway: "Shawna, you are a very talented student. Why not skip the PR thing, travel and immediately start a writing career?"

▶▶ 5-5: If you have seen the movie or read the *"Smoking"* book, how might you argue Shawna's point that Nick Naylor is not your typical PR practitioner?

▶▶ 5-6: It is true that the PR field has no requirements for entry. Does this fact bother the PR major? What about licensing (like accountants do with the CPA)?

Granted, those who have read the following case believe it is the silliest and most outlandish one in this book. OK, my colleagues in analysis, does that mean we ignore the case—that it's so silly and so unlikely that it doesn't deserve any kind of scrutiny? Not so fast, partners...

Case 6: Separate But Equal is Back? You've Got to be Joshin'!

You Tweak Your Resume and Get a PR Job

You are Josh Stewart Slightly "Stew"-Pidd. Your momma came from the Aryan Appalachian pioneer Slightly clan and your daddy from the Pidd pure-white bloodlines of Pennsylvania. Before he passed on, your daddy was active in politics as head of the Pidd Party of Pennsylvania, largely devoted to the "advancement of racial equality through strict separation."

It says on your resume you are a liberal studies graduate from David Duke University. Actually, you told your boss, Uncle Boss Pidd, you graduated, but you still have to retake a couple of classes to get your GPA up to the required 2.0 level. On your resume, you listed PR courses you hope to take eventually online, although the words "hope to take" were in very small print and likely were overlooked because your uncle needs reading glasses but is too vain to wear them (his girlfriend thinks they make the 62-year-old Boss look old). Anyway, your uncle (the boss) owns Impressive Visions Agency (IVA), and therefore you are offered a job as communications assistant for that small-but-growing public relations concern (currently you and Boss), located in an out-of-the-way area in the Smoky Mountains. The agency has recently landed a chance to pitch a big nonprofit client—an upstart with little identity and no previous record of promotions. IVA has been asked to give a pitch to the new nonprofit client. The best part of it all: The client will pay your agency $25,000 just to put together ideas for a pitch! No cattle call! Not a freebie! You are the first agency to get this pitch assignment. If you and Boss succeed, they will not go to any other agency. You'll have the account.

For Now: Low Profile, Please

For now, this client wants to remain a low-profile group, hoping to successfully resurrect and advocate your daddy's pet agenda: "Separate But Equal" (SBE). Their PR director tells you a reinvigorated SBE initiative will "bring a lot of good to this world and much more law and order to America." Separate But Equal wants to eventually enact national legislation to, as they put it, "strengthen legacy identities through bringing together various races and heritages to be concentrated 'in geographic exclusivity' in the United States."

SBE's PR director, Kris Kane-Kampf, is very excited about the first of what they hope are many "racial purity and homeland identity" initiatives: the use of federal tax breaks, housing allowances, special funds and military oversight to encourage people of various descent to live in geographic areas specially designated for what SBE calls "the enhancement and preservation of their proud heritage." Says, Kane-Kampf: "We believe a lot of trouble and crime in America is caused because various blood lines are separated and alienated internally. Bring like-minded and like-blooded people together and they will cease to undermine the national integrity. This has been proven time and time again throughout history."

She has suggested the Mexican Chistosos as your pitch racial target. You and Boss have been designated to come up with ideas to introduce an SBE Chistosos Pride initiative in the United States. SBE is sponsoring this experimental PR campaign to see "if we have the persuasive communication abilities to get the majority of Americans the United States behind the SBE movement. We believe there's an untapped majority faction of Americans out there that will love our ideas, particularly that self-governance and racial identity-building in geographic subdistricts is the key to a stronger, safer America," notes Kane-Kampf. "We just need to test it all with a dynamic, willing communications agency to make sure we're credible and convincing before we ever roll out any kind of billion-dollar campaign."

The SBE PR director suggests that something like the following be included in your experimental campaign pitch: "Humor! Maybe something playing on the Chistosos' propensity for sucking strong herb on a hookah, hitting the hot tub and then maybe shooting rifles in the air. Put a rollicking Chistosos bath/smoke house in an ad that introduces potential community-building SBE benefits to these rowdy immigrants in America. But also appeal to long-standing, regular Americans to support the same project," she says. She specifically chose your agency because of your reputed social media skills. "I don't care what the story is about. Your uncle sent me your resume, Josh, and I am very impressed with your social media skills. Just make sure that those Chistosos love your message and, well, those who don't particularly want the influx of Chistosos in their neighborhoods in all 50 states love it as well! We're trying to see if we can make both sides happy with our program: Real Americans can get their country back and new Americans can be safe and sound with their own kind. We're looking to put those Chistosos somewhere in Alaska, surrounded by a snow fort (that they will finance) in the permafrost. So if we like your approach, the next step will be focus groups to test your messages. After that, we expand our initiative with the Crustaceans of Guatemala, another group that's entering America in record numbers. "Just a bunch of hard-shelled dark-skinned druggies, if you ask me. But that's strictly off the record. Just like the Chistosos, we've got Crustaceans now in all 50 states. It's time they were all consolidated somewhere," says Kane-Kampf.

Therefore, you and Boss Pidd have ultimately been advised to use whatever communication strategy and creative information that works. SBE believes the experimental campaign could be successful because a variety of mass media are now fighting for advertising dollars to stay alive. Your uncle says most media will run ads that look very much like news stories, if the price is right. You are to prepare mock-ups of those prospective stories. If ultimately your Chistosos SBE campaign is well-received and initiatives are begun to finance and create snow fortified Chistosos enclaves in Alaska, the SBE assures Impressive Visions that they have "at least a dozen" other immigrant races to target and that Impressive Visions will "make big money" on all of those campaigns. "We just chose the Chistosos at random to see how a campaign might play out," notes Kane-Kampf. "Actually, you can do your pitch with the Crustaceans, if you want. Or try both at once. Get creative! And very persuasive—in an energizing, empathetic sort of way."

It Ain't Her Real Name

SBE leadership evidently has a lot of money to spend from many anonymous donors. Their entire operation does prefer, however, to remain very low profile. In fact, their marketing director actually goes by a pseudonym: Kris-Kane-Kampf. "It ain't my real name," she says. "And don't forget to stress that in America, it will be much easier for our government to communicate with races if we've got them geographically united." You tell her you are "all in favor of better communication between the government and various immigrant groups. You also tell her that you have taken quite a few courses on racial purity at Duke. She says she already knows that.

To you, it seems a doable task to first sell people on the Separate But Equal idea and then spend hundreds of millions of dollars to influence legislation that would begin the process of resettlement. Your boss agrees: "Every great idea has to start—or restart— sometime and somewhere. Let's get in on the ground floor of this one. They've hired Impressive Visions because we have the reputation of keeping quiet. We divulge nothing about our clients, particularly the overseas ones. And that's how it should be. Of course, this is currently just an experiment. It's all just hypocritical."

"Hypothetical," you say.

"That's the word!" And Boss laughs.

In one week, Uncle Boss wants a Facebook story that tells people how Chistosos and/or Crustacean community forces in America are rallying around the SBE effort and yearn to be united in the United States rather than scattered all over the map. "Put something in there about their willingness to wear name tags or have their names and race tattooed on their arms, Stew."

The next week, he wants to see a draft of a "United in the United States" advertorial that promotes the financial and social benefits of separate but equal racial identity communities and offers $500 'per head' for those who will have HITs (Heritage Identity Tattoos) applied to their arms.

And there is more! Boss also wants to advance a theory that folks like Chistosos and Crustaceans have "ancient Artic blood" in their genes. That's why both races are currently "confused" and causing problems, he notes. "Get them into their original, God-given habitat and watch how they flourish, Josh! OK, so I'm still working on getting some scientist to back me up on this theory, but we'll use it now and I'm sure sooner or later somebody will come along to verify it. Oh, and try to work a bible verse or two in your campaign materials."

For your consideration:

➡ 6-1: Stew, given your background, would you have any reservations about pitching this client at this juncture? If your agency doesn't pick up the lucrative pitch money, another agency certainly will. Besides, Boss says that if SBE likes the Impressive Visions campaign approach, he guarantees you a raise and a promotion within six months! (And it doesn't hurt that you are the only one who knows about Shirley, as you caught Boss nibbling on Shirley's ear when his wife was out of town.)

➡ 6-2: Is it right to "fudge" a bit on the resume? Don't you really need to do so to get ahead? Everybody does it, right? So your uncle thinks you actually graduated summa cum laude from Duke. So he thinks you actually took all those PR courses. So he thinks you can write. So maybe you did put "PR Major Best Righter Award" on your resume to "round it out" a little. Golly, he was actually thinking of hiring Shirley for the job. Dang, she's 17 and still in high school!

➡ 6-3: Is it really possible to use essentially the same message to appeal to different perspectives? Have your PR courses taught you to write powerful, energizing empathetic messages? If Stew's father can resurrect SBE, can the best PR practitioners resurrect the "magic bullet" or "hypodermic needle" effects of communication?

➡ 6-4: Identify the major premises and assumptions in this case. There are many. For example: the need to keep confidences regarding the sponsor of the message. In this case, is that good PR? Or consider this tactic: The advancing of theories that people might believe, but looking for support for that theory later. Or what about the plan to keep the races together to preserve their heritage? Or consider the tactic of putting together a war chest of money to promulgate stories about your cause, even if those stories are made up. After all, making up stories is OK if you are advancing the public good, right, Stew? And what about the practice of making paid advertising look like real news stories? Are you sure this case is all that far-fetched? Are you *sure* there are no Josh or Kris or Boss folks out there searching for credibility and adherents anymore?

▶▶ 6-5: Now suppose that Josh is an intelligent, dynamic communicator with a strong academic background and a passion to achieve in the PR field. Does that change anything?

Case 7: You Want Great Art or Do You Want to Pay the Bills?

You Have a Great Job While in College

Most of your fellow students at Quad Cities State work in fast food or retail to make extra money for expenses. You, Lenny "The Lens" Lucasey, get 25 hours a week at a PR agency—and at twice the money the average college student makes. You consider yourself very fortunate to have landed such a position, particularly since the agency schedules all of your assignments around your class commitments. True, some of the bigger agencies have at least one full-time script and shoot and edit guru, but Quad Communications (QC) is a small operation that succeeds by using part-timers like you. The bigger agencies have to bill at least twice the fee for the same services you provide. And you believe that the quality of your complete video services is just as good as theirs. Your boss at QC, Franklin Mint, believes that, too.

It is the first semester of your senior year. Quad Cities State does not offer public relations. Nor does it offer any kind of video or broadcast curriculum. So in terms of PR knowledge, you are largely self-taught. And in terms of video, you went to a large high school that had better equipment and better teachers than many American universities do. In high school, you were known as the school's top "lens geek." Most of your free time was devoted to learning how to script, shoot and edit. By the time you graduated, you had won several awards for your videography, one of them a national competition with a $1,000 first prize.

So why would you choose QC? To be honest, your girlfriend was enrolled there. Ironically, you two broke up before the end of your first semester. She objected to your shooting of what you call a "tastefully erotic" short video. You told her that video was your life and that you needed to "follow your muse" without any interference. That ended the relationship. Also, you chose QC so you could save money and live at home. As a commuter, you do save a lot. Third, QC has reputedly one of the best marketing departments in the Midwest. Your high school mentor told you that most universities could "not really improve much" on your video skills, so that QC was a good choice, since you needed to learn as much as possible about business and marketing. This advice turned out to be beneficial. As a senior, you are very happy. And very busy. No time for a girlfriend. No time to party. You carry a 3.9/4.0 grade average and are president of the QC Marketing Club. And, of course, you have your commitment to Mr. Mint and Quad Communications. Yes, life is good.

Full Control of an Important Project

"Lens, we now have enough work to bring you on full-time, and with a significant raise," Mint tells you. He knows for certain, however, that you will not quit school with less than a year to go. But he is already, as he says it, "putting in our bid for the best talent around these parts." True, you have toyed with the idea of heading to Chicago to work for a large agency after graduation, and Mint knows this. What he doesn't know is that your dad is ill and cannot work anymore. You intend to remain at home with him and your mom, as you are very close to both. You tell yourself that QC Communications can offer you plenty of the creative challenges you need after graduation. However, your next assignment soon casts considerable doubt on that notion.

The Eastern Iowa Health Coalition (EIHC) has hired Quad Communications to do a video that will be accessible to all 79 of its member institutions: hospitals, physician practices and many other healthcare concerns in a 20-county area. Among its other duties, the Coalition lobbies in Des Moines. Lately, EIHC has been criticized by some of its members as ineffectual in terms of influencing legislation favorable to the healthcare industry. EIHC president Sherwood Witcomb "Witty" Shoen is livid. He wants to prove that EIHC does have an impact in Des Moines. Shoen's six-person staff consists of a marketing consultant, legal consultant, IT consultant, a lobbyist, a shared purchases coordinator and an executive assistant. He does not have a designated PR person, however. Shoen says, "I do all our PR. And I know what I want. I want to be on camera to show our dues-paying members just how hard we work!" So Shoen hires Quad Communications to do a video called "Eastern Iowa Health Coalition Under Witty Shoen: We Do Get Results in Des Moines!" Mr. Mint gives you full control of the project.

On the Phone with Witty Shoen

"Well, I don't have a lotta extra time, and I know exactly what I want in this video, but I guess we could do a quick lunch somewhere so I could answer your questions," Shoen tells you on the phone. You called to tell him it is important that the videographer develops a good rapport with his client and thoroughly researches the client's needs. You further state that although you have already done considerable research on the Eastern Iowa Health Coalition, you really need some of his insights before you prepare this important public relations tactic.

"Videographer? Is that what Minty is calling you to pad the price?" he says, chuckling.

"Well, sir, actually the QC prices for a complete video treatment are about half of what they'd be if your organization were based in Chicago."

"Wouldn't make much sense to headquarter an Eastern Iowa healthcare association in Chicago, now would it?" He laughs again. You laugh, too. Then you agree on a date and a restaurant. He says, "I presume this lunch is on your expense account, right, junior shooter?" He will call you "junior shooter" throughout the process of creating his video.

Meeting with Witty and Biddie

You arrive a few minutes early at the restaurant. Shoen is already seated. You recognize him from the photo used in a recent annual report. In person, he looks about 10 years older than the photo image. Late 50s. Bald. Gray scruff on face. And not alone. He has brought along his executive assistant, Bidwell Curtz. You button your suit coat, straighten your tie and proceed to meet them and shake hands. It isn't long before you discover that what Biddie wants, Biddie gets. She offers a limp hand and gets right down to business:

45

"Mr. Shoen and I know exactly what we need," she tells you. Then she gives you a look that seems to be more of a salacious leer than a simple assessment of your posture and professional deportment. "You're the handsome kid they sent to shoot us, right? Or are you taking our lunch order?" Witty Shoen laughs heartily, much too heartily in your estimation: "That's a good one, Biddie!" You have already heard through the grapevine that they, although both married to other people, are intimate. She started out as a secretary with Shoen ten years ago. They say that now she runs the entire operation. As you seat yourself, she plops on your plate a stack of papers that resemble a script.

"This is your script," she tells you. "Now before your boss buys me the prime rib, what exactly do you need to know?"

You take pride in the fact that you are not the pretentious type. But you are getting a bit irritated. Maybe it's time to show these old fuddy duddies that you know your stuff: "Well, we want to go for the most impact with your target audience, so let's start by discussing your objectives for this video project."

"Witty has but one objective: to get those frigging whiners off our backs. We do plenty in Des Moines, as this here script clearly shows."

"I look forward to reading it," you say. You quickly rifle through the contents, noting that it is all "talking heads," mostly Shoen and Curtz. You try not to cringe as you realize that if all this is shot, the video will run at least 30 minutes.

"Interesting assertion," you say, as you quote Schoen on page 13: "The state wants to tax certain nonessential medical procedures? We'll fight that to the death!" Then you ask, "For example, what kind of illustrative video would you want to accompany that? I presume we go for specific medical procedures to shoot."

"B-roll? Yeah, I know the jargon," says Witty.

"And we'll have none of that crap," Curtz quickly adds. "It's all only window dressing—distraction—for those speakers who can't hold an audience. Me and Witty, we can. It's all us. All the time. And we're sure we can hold our members mesmerized. They like us. Do you like that word, Witty?"

You aren't hungry anymore. Your clients devour their meals quickly as you pretend to peruse their script. Oh, and you wish you could do something about Shoen's voice. It is strident and hardly reassuring.

"Looking forward to your shooting. We'll practice so we do it in one take," says Shoen as he gets up to leave and shoves the check in your direction. "QC is charging by the hour. Healthcare concerns are always being criticized for spending way too much money, so we want to nip those costs in the bud!" His voice and jargon remind you of Barney Fife.

A Sit-down with Mr. Mint

Bringing the restaurant check immediately back to QC is a good excuse to try to see Mr. Mint as soon as possible. He is in a meeting, but he does finally emerge and find time for a short conversation.

"How'd it go with Witty and Biddie, champ? This ought to be an easy one, huh?"

"Easy in what respect, Mr. Mint?"

"Slam! Bam! In the can! What do they want in terms of your scripting?"

"Nothing. They already wrote the script." You toss the bound papers on your boss's desk. Maybe you threw them down a bit too hard.

A quick flip through the script and Mint readily sees your problem. "Any way they'll let you do some creative b-roll, or can you get them to break up their explanations into more than just sit-on-your-butt-and-talk scenarios? We could get some good background of those two walking hospital hallways."

"You already know the answer, right?"

"Yeah," says Mint, dropping his head. "You're just there to record at least a half hour of talking heads. And I bet they won't want any editing. Just let the camera roll and roll and roll... Lemme show you an email I just got from Biddie..."

Minty! Thanks for the scrumptious lunch! Your cameraman is young. Good-looking, too! But as long as he does what he's told, we'll wrap this up in no time. Witty and I got the idea that he either wanted to cut down the speeches and/or add some visuals while we talked. None of that is going to happen. We've got thirty minutes of what we believe is compelling evidence to show that our organization kicks ass in Des Moines. Send the kid over as soon as you can and we'll get this done!

Then You Say It

"Mr. Mint, with all due respect, I can't do this."

"Look, this is strictly business. You're a smart guy who is studying business. Get it shot and forget about it. It doesn't have to go in your portfolio."

"I cannot give a client anything that is clearly sub-standard. Do they really think even their most loyal of members will last 30 seconds, let alone 30 minutes with this snoozer? And don't they realize they'll be laughed at by anyone who knows the least bit about videography and advocacy?"

"That's not our problem. We give the client what he wants. Sure, we recommend, we try to make improvements. But we also know when to back off and collect that important paycheck. Hey, do you want to make great art or do you want to pay your bills? Now set up a time to shoot and get the damn thing done!"

For your consideration:

▸▸ 7-1: Is the client "always right"?

▸▸ 7-2: Do you say anything more to your boss after he tells you to get the job done? What about: "I thought you said I had FULL CONTROL of the project?"

▸▸ 7-3: Is it time to rethink your plans and look into jobs in Chicago? Will it be any different there?

▸▸ 7-4: You do decide to "get it over with." As Biddie and you wait for Shoen to join you in the conference room where you will shoot, she winks and pinches your behind.

Some students are impressive. Michelle is one of those. She is very ambitious and undaunted when it comes to tasks that others consider "nearly impossible." But this time, maybe reality wins out?

Case 8: Your First Job: Save Summer School

They Like You!

On December 1, just before taking finals, you, Michelle Vasco-Degamma, call your parents and ask them if the extra bed is still available in the basement. They ask you if you have applied for jobs yet. Yes, you had applied for one: an on-campus position, full-time, year-round with benefits, as Summer School Marketing Assistant. You tell them that competition for that job is likely to be fierce, but the good news is that you got a "screening" interview on the day you have no final exams so, at least, this would be good interviewing practice. According to your sources, they are screening the applicant pool down to five people or fewer, expecting to interview a dozen on the phone. "I'll be applying for many positions once finals are finished," you tell your parents. "I do feel fortunate just to have made the cut to the top 12. On the other hand, my strong GPA, graduating a semester early, a great internship with Tarhelia State Admissions, my presidency of PRSSA and my year as student government PR liaison give me an advantage over a lot of other students looking for their first jobs. Overall, I'm optimistic."

Screening Via Skype Lasts 15 minutes. You Think You Did Well.

It does get better. On the day of your last final exam, Harold Matriculus, director of Summer School at your school, Tarhelia State, calls to tell you that they want to interview you again—this time in person, as you are one of four finalists. He tells you that if hired, you would be in charge of competing against the "daunting" tuition grant that Tarhelia State implemented with special state funding last semester. What seems daunting to the head of the summer school program seems a godsend to Tarhelia State Admissions. T-State is one of two North Carolina universities that the legislature chose to get tuition assistance (the "TAP" Tuition Assistance Program legislation) for the next three years. One big reason your school was chosen: diversity. You have a student population that is 34 percent minorities. While other state schools charge about $3,000 per semester for tuition, first semester of the new program, applications to T-State quadrupled!

The problem: The $750 charge (it averages about $50 per credit) only pertains to the two, regular semesters. Summer school is not included. The current tuition rate per credit for summer school is $220, more than four times the tuition assistance rate. In your interview, Matriculus and Reggie Star, his Coordinator of the Summer Schedule, make it clear that summer school "is on its own; we must pay our own way or die." They note that about 20 percent of those attending summer school come from the teaching professions, so those students are not likely to balk at the tuition difference, particularly since their schools tend to pay at least part of the tuition. "But that other 80 percent," notes Matriculus, "is largely undergrads, most coming from our own student body. How can we possibly convince them not to skip summer school in favor of the much lower tuition in the regular semesters?"

That, indeed, was a tough question. Evidently, they must have liked your answer. You got the job.

Four Months to Sell the Summer: Research First

Your first day on the job, Matriculus tells you a big reason you got the job was because you are well-known among the 10,000 students who attend Tarhelia State, particularly since your blog and video series, "What's Student Government Done for you Lately?" was quite popular. "We hope you can translate that credibility and popularity into summer school enrollment," he says.

"I consider it a challenge I intend to meet," you reply.

What to do first? Your PR studies have convinced you that research is essential before you implement tactics. So you schedule eight focus groups to be held the first two weeks of February. You will then use data from those focus groups to do a survey of the student body.

What You Discovered

A. Most of the students in the focus groups and those who responded to the survey were *not aware* that the tuition assistance program did not include summer school. You immediately went to work to inform campus media about that. Then, the student-run newspaper, the student-run radio station

51

and the student-run weekly TV news program all gave extensive coverage regarding that tuition discrepancy.

B. Most of your research respondents reacted very negatively to the news that summer school was not covered under the three-year, legislature-mandated tuition cut. In fact, after they found out about this problem, various student groups, including Student Congress, took action. They petitioned the administration for summer-school tuition parity. They sent a delegation to Raleigh. There was even a brief sit-in in the provost's office after the provost issued the following statement:

As much as I would love to see summer tuition be the same as tuition for our regular semesters, the legislature has no intention of including summer tuition in their TAP (Tuition Assistance Program). The fact is that even at $220 per credit, traditionally summer school operates in the red. We actually lose money each summer. So we are already doing a public service by keeping summer tuition low and by offering classes that are needed but are not profitable.

What Happens Next?

Will faculty members be willing to take a cut in summer school pay to reduce the $220 per-credit charge? Not likely. According to your boss, the newly formed faculty union would never consent to that.

How about cancelling classes with low enrollment? Matriculus tells you that such an austerity measure is already in place. The best they can hope for is that mass lecture classes in the summer fill up. Then they might be able to reduce the cost of tuition for those classes. Then again, many departments depend on large enrollments in mass lectures so they can offer special summer classes with low enrollments. "Not much wiggle room with that one, either, I'm afraid," he says. "We've got to sell summer and the $220 per credit that is pretty much set in stone," he tells you. We've got to find a way to change the negative attitude toward the relatively high summer tuition. That won't be easy. And, as you know, just because attitude changes does not mean that action follows. Even those who may agree that summer is still a relative bargain and convenient in order to enroll in otherwise-hard-to-get courses, won't necessarily enroll for summer courses here at Tarhelia State."

For your consideration:

➡ 8-1: The boss is relying on your reputation and your social media skills to help keep Summer School from dying. What are you prepared to do? Isn't this a lot to ask of an entry-level practitioner?

➡ 8-2: Are you feeling a lot of pressure? How do you intend to handle that pressure?

➡ 8-3: You still have all of March and April to promote summer school classes. It's eight weeks before Maymester and then two, six-week sessions to follow. All departments have submitted their summer school course schedules. They are offering about the same number of courses that they did last summer. Evidently, they don't foresee a big drop in demand. Or, perhaps, they don't want to foresee that. What can you do at the department level to promote summer school?

➡ 8-4: You have learned in your various classes that PR is not a panacea. PR people cannot perform miracles. Is it time to make some realistic projections on how much summer school attendance will drop? Your research shows that the majority of respondents who took summer classes last year (72 percent) agree or strongly agree that they will postpone summer classes this year, even if it means taking an extra semester. How will you prepare all key publics for a letdown?

➡ 8-5: By the way, your job has been funded for one year only. What do you believe are REASONABLE performance expectations for your position? How will you communicate that to your boss?

Case 9: When You Follow the Act of a Saint

They Only Want Michelle

Every time you hear the name Michelle Vasco-Degamma you want to scream! (and sometimes "regurgitate," to be totally honest). You, Judy Suite-Blueyes, have been doing your internship for only two days at Tarhelia State Admissions (four hours per day in the summer for three days a week for eight weeks when the internship is completed), and you have heard that name perhaps, conservatively speaking, a billion times already. "Michelle did it this way…" "Michelle always said…" "Maybe you will want to call Michelle before you do that; she's on campus over at Summer School…"

OK, you are ready to concede that Michelle Vasco-Degamma was and will always be the finest intern ever to serve in the Admissions Department. Everyone in the department has told you that over and over and over…Will they ever get OVER her? What can you possibly do to make that happen?

Take an assessment of yourself, Judy. True, your GPA is two one-hundredths of a point lower than Michelle's when she graduated. True, Michelle is considered the finest PRSSA president ever to serve at T-State. You? A forgettable vice-president, even though you headed a Bateman team that did very well last year. In fact, you saved Michelle's overcommitted butt by editing and finishing the visuals for her part of the presentation on deadline. And leadership? Michelle was the darling of Student Congress. You: a mere representative for Pan-Hel. Oh, and you need the credits from this internship to graduate in summer. Eight semesters and one summer. Michelle did it in seven semesters. Plus, Michelle was nominated to Homecoming Court. She has been deemed "beautiful." You? Cute. Just "cute."

Eighty-eight clock hours to go before you hear the last of Michelle at your internship. Even your interactions with the professor who recommended you for the internship are disheartening. You saw Dr. Philbin Regis in the hallway yesterday. What did he ask? "How is the Michelle internship going?" Not how is YOUR Admissions internship going! Michelle Vasco-Degamma has been sanctified and enshrined in the Tarhelia State Admissions Office. And then the dream last night. The most popular admissions counselor on staff, Steve Studly, asks if you don't mind taking on a special project. He wants you to sculpt a bust of Michelle to put in the Admissions entryway. "You were an art minor, right, Julie?" he says. You might have a bit of a crush on him. But don't bother. He's probably patiently standing in line to get a date with Michelle. After all, he doesn't even know your first name.

Frustrated for Sure

Are you bitter? A bit jealous? Frustrated. Frustrated for sure. Does anyone in the office remember that during your internship interview you said you actually want to work in university admissions? That you think you'd LOVE the contact with prospective students? Would anyone there believe that Saint Michelle the Beautiful once confided that her admissions internship "was not going to lead to anything, just a good recommendation." In fact, she found admissions work "a bit on the boring side." Really.

Maybe the best course of action would be to drop the internship. Eight hours already invested on the job. At first you were given an interesting task: editing the monthly Admissions newsletter and writing a key feature story for it. Then, suddenly, two hours into the challenging project and the V.P. of Admissions comes around to your desk and takes the assignment away! For what reason? The story involves summer admissions recruitment of summer school students from other campuses. "Since Michelle is working closely with us now, I'll have her write the feature. And while she's at it, I'm sure she won't mind editing the newsletter, too. Here, I've got a huge mailing list database that I need to be cross-referenced with names and graduation dates from Alumni Affairs. You can get started on that instead, Judy."

Time to go see your internship supervisor, Dr. Regis. Tell him your reservations about ever making anything more out of this internship than a passable bust of Michelle and producing a clean mailing database, a cleaning task that may take all 88 hours to complete.

Surprise!

You used to think that Dr. Regis was a sweetheart of a guy. Well, he did listen when you went to see him. Then he reacted:

"Judy, nobody is expecting you to be another Michelle. I think you need to suck it up and strive to contribute something unique to Admissions, like Michelle did."

LIKE MICHELLE DID? He really said that.

"Any ideas what I might try to accomplish to set me apart, Dr. Regis?"

"Well, I don't know that job very well. Talk to somebody who can give you insights. I'm thinking maybe you should sit down with…" Michelle. Yes, he said, "Michelle"!

For your consideration:

▶▶ 9-1: Are you in the wrong situation? Tarhelia does not require the internship to earn the PR degree. You still have time to take a summer course, get those credits and graduate. Would that be better?

▶▶ 9-2: Of course, you truly are interested in admissions work. Michelle claims that admissions reps are "just glorified salespeople." Nonetheless, you would be selling something you truly believe in: higher education. Except for being in the shadow of Michelle, you have loved your time at Tarhelia, and you believe you could represent very well a lot of different schools in North Carolina. Of course, without any kind of admissions experience at all, who would hire you? Well, you were an ambassador. That should help the job search.

➨ 9-3: Are you forgettable? You were an Admissions Ambassador all last year. You gave at least a dozen tours for prospective students and their parents. One time, however, Michelle came by with her group as you were explaining the historical and symbolic significance of the bell tower in the Quad. Michelle started in on her explanation. Damn! Your crowd moved closer to hear her! And then they followed HER for the rest of the tour. So you followed them. Why follow the cute one when you can follow the beautiful one? And did Dr. Regis REALLY suggest that you go see Michelle? (He did.)

You, Jason, have a tendency to be a bit confrontational, although you do not mean to always be so abrasive. It's just that you like to cut through the rhetoric and get to the truth. However, Hydra finally has had enough of you, as she thinks you go way too far in questioning a gracious and generous potential employer.

Case 10: It's Tempting, but is it Really PR?

Hydra Shows Her Email at the PRSSA Meeting

You, Jason Argonaut, and 13 other PR majors at Coastal Kansas University are decidedly all on edge. You all will graduate in five weeks, and you all want those public relations jobs that CKU recruiters told you when you were freshmen would be "plentiful in four short years." Yes, there are jobs, but "plentiful" they are not.

The night of the third-to-last PRSSA meeting of the spring semester, PRSSA President Hydra Sidewinder has a brief presentation to make. She calls it "PR Seniors: Let's Get to Work!" She opens the presentation with an email she received from the president of a new company, VCSD: Virtual Cyber Software Developers:

Hey, Hydra! Thank you so much for speaking with me on the phone last week! And, again, congratulations on being a leader in the academic PR field. It became instantly clear to me that you indeed have the intelligence, education and drive to succeed in a public relations position at dynamic (and growing exponentially every day!) VCSD. I am so glad you saw our ad online and called me for more information. What a pleasure it is to talk to the future communication talent that is sure to bring VCSD prestige and lucrative salaries for its PR professionals. I would like to invite you to a dinner so you can meet our leadership. It will be an informational dinner, as by then I will have prepared full answers to the many insightful questions you asked me on the phone. As you know, we are just getting started here at VCSD. Therefore, after the dinner and presentation, I would like to meet with you privately so that you can critique my PR presentation. I was an IT major a few years ago, and now I realize I could have *benefited from taking some PR classes. So your candid critique will be most helpful. In exchange, it's a free dinner at Chez Gruel, a Kansas City restaurant I sure couldn't afford when I was an undergrad! We will also cover your transportation costs, since Coastal Kansas is a good hour away from Chez Gruel. In fact, bring all other soon-to-graduate PR cohorts. Their ticket to a four-star meal will be their resumes. And they too will get a stipend to cover transportation costs. Whether you carpool or not, each of you will get a check for $50. In fact, this may turn into a kind of focus group, as our leadership is eager to pick your PR brains for ideas! I will call you in a few days to determine how many Coastal Kansas Great Plains Surfers (GPS! I love that name!) to expect at a dinner that will change their lives—and not just for the better—but for THE BEST. Virtual Cyber Software Developers is THE BEST. If you have what it takes, come do PR for THE BEST.*

-- All THE BEST, Harold "Huck" Yahoo

What an Enthusiastic Hydra Tells Your PRSSA Group:

"Huck sounded SO NICE on the phone. Personally, I'm going to drive to K.C. and get that free meal and stipend. What do I have to lose? It's a new company that is developing software that people can use on their computers and mobile devices. It's virtual reality software without any wires or goggles—nothing but air between your device and your virtual experience. I don't know a lot more about the technology, but I do know that Huck says he needs communicators who can "advance the idea." We all know that one function of PR is to be on the cutting edge of communicating new developments that some people might consider odd or unreal. Huck says virtual reality software that requires no hardware is one of those bold ideas that needs to seek out public acceptance from those with money to invest but who aren't necessarily among the early adopter types. I'm going to find out more. Free dinner and 50 bucks. I've got to call Huck in two days to tell him how many seats to save at the table two weeks from tomorrow. Anyone want to join me?"

Of course, being PR majors, we were full of questions, most of which Hydra could not answer. She kept responding, "Dunno for sure. That's why I'm taking the next step and going to the dinner!"

Consulting a Mentor Before the Trip

Of the 13 soon-to-graduate PRSSA members, ten of you sign up for the dinner. You, Jason, are skeptical. In fact, you refer to the freebie as a "time share pitch for condos on the Kansas Coast." That gets a big laugh. You also say that "VCSD sounds like some kind of social disease!" That also gets a big laugh, but not such a big one from Hydra.

It takes a lot to impress you. Unlike most of your peers, you did not grow up in small-town Kansas. You are a K.C. guy from an upper middle class neighborhood not far from Chez Gruel. So the first thing you do after Hydra's presentation is to consult your PR professor and academic adviser, Quinten Quaint. He is also from K.C. Quaint listens to you explain the dinner/stipend offer and then offers this: "Jay, why not go investigate? What are your plans for Saturday night? Cheeseburgers and a few brewskis? I think you've got a better offer now. You should check out the company. They do have an office and do seem legit. They belong to a chamber of commerce and the Better Business Bureau has nothing on them. And you already know that Chez Gruel is a classy place. Besides, you'll have plenty of company in case they have ulterior motives. I doubt if these software developers plan to kidnap all ten of you and sell you into slavery! Be discerning. Be skeptical. Ask questions. But I'd advise you to check it out."

Lobster and Filet Mignon for Ten

So you all stuff resumes into manila folders and large envelopes, fill two cars and head for K.C. on an April Saturday night. You have to admit it: These might be computer geeks, but they sure know how to throw a time-share party! The big surprise: It turns out that Hydra was more than a post-event critical consultant.

It turns out that Huck employed her to develop the theme of the dinner. So when Huck introduced himself during the mocktails pre-dinner gathering, he said, "Hydra and I wanted this to be a surprise. I'm not an expert at special events. Clearly, that's one of Hydra's strengths. So I empowered her to promote VCSD at this dinner. And in additional to the theme of THE BEST that she created and used on cocktail napkins, she'll also have a few words to share later in the program. Oh, and we paid her, of course. Five hundred dollars. Of course, she refused it initially. Then she suggested that the money be a donation to your PRSSA chapter to offset costs involved in your upcoming Batman competition in Dallas."

"Bateman." You, Jason, quickly correct Huck, your virgin daiquiri quivering in your hand. You adjust your clip-on tie like Rodney Dangerfield.

"Of course, Jason! Bateman! Thank you!"

Impressive. Maybe Huck was just joking around. The impressive part: He already knew your name. No nametags. You had just entered the room minutes ago. And Hydra, looking natty in the blue business suit she got from her parents at Christmas is laughing: "Huck loves that joke!" she says. She looks so grown up and professional.

The food was wonderful.

What Did We Learn?

For one thing, Jason, you, learned that there is a difference between asking an incisive question and an obnoxious one. At least Hydra thought you went over the line of good taste, and she ranted about that all the way home in the car, reportedly calling YOU a "social disease." You weren't in that car. You were on the way down, but you switched to the other car on the way back, fearing the wrath of Hydra. Your first transgression: Among the perks of the job, Huck noted that "those chosen for our PR slots get their own offices." Your hand went up: "Uh, now you computer geeks do know the difference between a telemarketer's cubicle and a PR practitioner's office, right, Huck?"

Huck was gracious. "Well, Jason, we'd be happy to show you five vacant offices we have in our facility now, all with doors and walls and windows. Guaranteed!"

Later, the other four occupants of Hydra's car would not divulge details. They just told you the next day that she used "language they had never heard from her before" in relation to your cubicle question. Of course, that probably wasn't the worst question you asked. When Huck said the new PR hires could earn "up to $100,000 their first year," your hand went up again: "Is that real money or Monopoly money?"

Ouch. And Hydra wasn't the only PRSSA member to flash you the hairy eyeball on that one.

Apart from your two (actually, THREE) blunt questions, here is what you also learned that night:

A. Huck admitted that the $100,000 would be a "share in the company." He noted, "It's the exact same share we are offering to those potential partners smart enough to get on board with our company. In the meantime, as you perfect your PR skills, we will give you a draw on that stock share: plenty of money for you to live on until you reach the $100,000 goal.

B. "That $100,00 goal and the salary draw arrangement seems more than fair," Hydra commented. "We all expect to earn our way to the top. It's kind of like a law firm, right? You earn your partnership with stellar work. Could you go into more detail on what would be our specific responsibilities to earn that partnership, Huck?" Huck deferred to his boss, Yates Yeehaw. Yates looked so much like Bill Gates. Uncanny! It's as if they went out to find a doppelganger and suit him up for the proceedings. Yates said, "It's all up to you. You are the PR experts. We do expect you to do plenty of media interface. We need the publicity to draw in potential partners. And we do expect you each to use your own, unique creative approaches to campaigning. We'll set you up with key publics who have been meticulously screened as potential partners. Our goal in the next year is to bring at least 500 potential partners on board."

C. OK, maybe you got in a third "shot." "Mr. Yeehaw, isn't it important that the company plan and adopt a uniform PR strategy rather than implement the various tactics of a variety of PR folks? Public relations theory would seem to dictate that."

D. Yates did not have the patience or the smile of Yahoo: "You tell *me*, Jordon," Yates Yeehaw snapped. Then Huck Yahoo took over again: "Some incisive questioning, Jason. We'll talk more after the dessert."

For your consideration:

➤➤ 10-1: Actually, Huck Yahoo completely avoided you after the dessert. So did Yates Yeehaw. And Hydra Sidewinder.

➤➤ 10-2: You return to your PR professor and a few days later give him a rundown of the dinner. He tells you that three of your PR peers have already signed up for interviews at the Kansas City VCSD facility. Is that your next step?

➤➤ 10-3: You do wonder about the legality of working to recruit "partners." Wouldn't you need some kind of stock broker license to do that? You also wonder if the PR people are to provide communications support (media releases, speech texts, brochures, online advertising) for the salespeople or if the PR people themselves are the salespeople. So you email Huck with that question. His response: *Hi, Jason! We've already hired our first three PR people, but we'll keep your resume on file for a year. Thanks for your continuing interest in THE BEST.*

➤➤ 10-4: Would it help or hurt to contact Hydra now?

What's wrong with contentment? People strive for it all their lives—and you've already achieved it at age 24. Sure, the money is bad, but you love what you do. Granted, it's a low-pressure, self-paced job and you work alone, Dirk. You like working alone. You are a bit concerned it does not bother you that you seem to lack ambition to climb the professional ladder, but certainly not concerned enough to immediately do anything about it...

Case 11: Is it Time to Shoot Again at the Professor's Target?

More than a Babysitter

If Professor Eon Jelloblock taught you one thing, it was to be patient in your quest for a great PR job. In fact, Jelloblock taught you a lot more than one thing, but his "target lecture" certainly remains at the forefront of the brain. He draws a target on the dry erase board, the kind an archer might use. It has a bullseye and four other sectors, with each outlying sector from the bullseye bigger than the last in area. Then he labels the bullseye "Perfect PR Position." The next sector out is labelled "Position in Communications Field." The third: "Some Professional Duties but not PR or Communications." The outside sector of the target is: "Fast food/retail." Then he tells you that upon graduation most of you will be given one arrow to shoot at a distance of 50 feet.* "How many of you will hit the bullseye on that single try?"

His point: Don't expect to graduate and find the perfect PR job immediately. There are jobs, but there is also stiff competition. More and more students enter university PR programs each year. "One day," he predicts, "we'll have many more students educated in PR than there are jobs. And, in some geographic locations, it will be tough to get that entry-level PR job even today. But don't give up!" You have not given up. It has been two years since you graduated with a PR degree. Your one "arrow" hit "kind of on the border" of sectors two and three. You work 35 hours a week at a radio station—actually two stations, both automated. Your hours suck (midnight to 5 a.m. seven days a week) but you like the feeling of being the only one in the broadcast building at those times. Your duties include the recording of weather information for the country station and the classic rock station. You also do the voice-overs for more than half of the local commercials that are inserted into the mix in both stations. The head of sales for both stations has said you've "got the right pipes" for the sounds of her stations and that she "hopes you stay forever." You feel that observation regarding your voice gives you a bit of job security.

When you were hired two years ago, the program director for both stations assured you that "you're in line for a lot more than this glorified babysitting gig, Pipes. Our promotions director is ambitious and certainly headed to one of our bigger sister stations in the Milwaukee market. And I think it will be soon. Pay your dues, play your cards right and be patient in this job and you'll get that PR position."

You are Happy, Dirk "Pipes" Burglar. Exceedingly

That's your on-air name and your nickname. Funny, but you've never really had to use it. Seldom do weather readers and commercial voices ever need to use their names. But one thing is clear: After two years, you still enjoy your job. Of course, at the outset, you didn't hit the bullseye. In fact, you are right on the borderline of "communication position" and "professional non-communication position," although your girlfriend and roommate, Joey Angelina, teases you that "your job is closer to fast food/retail on Jelloblock's target—except it doesn't pay as well!"

She jests, but there is a modicum of truth in her humor. Eight bucks an hour and no benefits. Student loans to continue to pay off. Whatever mileage to be gotten from this job for the resume has been achieved already. Jelloblock says that after two years in a position, if you have been successful, you are given a second arrow and moved 25 feet closer to the target. Of course, you have been *given* the arrow. What you choose to do with it is up to you. So far, it still lies on the ground. "Pick it up, put it on the bow and give it a shot!" Joey urges. She graduated a year before you and has a full-time job with benefits as an insurance salesperson. Last year she made four times what you did.

Here's the rub: You are happy. With your work hours, you get to see Joey a lot. In fact, you want to ask her to marry you. Believe it or not, you do not suffer from male jealousy. You are proud she makes a lot of money. So why go for another job? Someday maybe that promotions coordinator will take another job. However, you are in no hurry for her to do so. In fact, you are not even sure that you want that position now – or later. And it turns out that your notion of being "a people person" that helped you choose PR just doesn't hold up. You like working alone. In addition, you like working in a self-paced job that is relatively pressure-free.

For your consideration:

➡ 11-1: You'll need to determine if there is any real seriousness to Joey's teasing. Could she love a husband who actually doesn't want to move closer to the target and shoot another arrow? She knows you love to cook for her. She knows how much you care for her. And she senses that you are happy.

➡ 11-2: So many people are discontent when it comes to their jobs. But not you. Do you lack ambition? Will you regret that later?
*Jelloblock does acknowledge that upon graduation, some PR majors, the ones with strong GPAs, excellent internship performance, comprehensive portfolios, great recommendations and PRSSA leadership background will "likely get two arrows and get to move many extra feet forward when they take their initial shots. But these are in the minority," he says.

Case 12: First Day on the Job for the PR Assistant: Where's the Boss?

It's Nothing Like a Sitcom

Remember that classic Seinfeld episode where George shows up for work at a sales job that he was never really offered? Since his "boss" is on vacation, George settles in for a week and does nothing, although he is supposedly working assiduously in his closed-door office on the Penske file. Well, that's the loony world of sitcom jobs. Your situation is the opposite. You have been hired as a PR assistant at Nosocomial Hospital, DuBois, Iowa. You, D. Julian Towershot, fresh out of the PR major at the University of Iowa with a minor in healthcare administration, report to work the first day to discover that your boss has been "missing" for a week. Nobody knows where he is. He left work a week ago Monday but has not been seen anywhere in town since. You are shown to your office, excited to get started, as the now-missing boss, George Cosmo Newman, told you two weeks ago he was "so relieved to finally have some help. Things are crazy around here in terms of PR commitments," he said. "Sometimes I just want to jump on a Mississippi paddleboat and head for the gulf. Ha! Glad you have so much spirit and energy, Julian. So very glad!"

You may have heard the phrase regarding "the fecal matter engaging the oscillatory mechanism." It does the very first minute you are on the job at Nosocomial. The secretary that PR shares with the Office of Development, Mary Richards, has placed a list of to-dos on your desk. "It's stuff that Mr. Newman hasn't gotten around to doing. I guess you'd better dig in until we find him."

"I guess I won't have a George Costanza kind of week," you tell Mary, chuckling. "So don't bother getting me the Penske file." She evidently is not familiar with the reference, so she just smiles and nods.

Mary Lists the Biggies

You discover that Mary is adept at keeping track of things. She knows what needs to be done but, of course, she has no background in PR. Still, as you look over the long list, you hope she'll be able to give you the necessary background so you can address each task with some semblance of confidence and prioritize what looks like an intimidating agenda. You call her memo:

Her Dirty Dozen

1. Development Department close to wooing big bucks from a wealthy donor. He's the manager of a local casino. Lunch today with Development Director Nickles and this big donor. Millikan Cookies will be there, too, as that fatso never misses a free meal. Nickles needs you to convince donor that if donor gives $3 million for a treatment facility for gambling addicts that the facility will receive constant media attention. Be sure to promise major, ongoing media coverage. Cookies and Nickles were counting on Mr. Newman to assure Raul Lette, that big donor, of bigtime media.

2. Photographer from *Herald-Telegraph* to shoot babies in neo-natal unit for feature story on the upgraded facility. I think Mr. Newman was supposed to contact parents to get signed release forms, but I don't have them in my files yet.

3. Yet another push by outsiders to get our hospital employees to unionize. Hospital administrator Cookies (fatso snob referred to above) just sent another voice mail to Mr. Newman's inbox this morning. Cookies sure sounded angry. "Where the hell's the speech you were supposed to write for me to address why unionization is bad for hospitals, Newman? I need it by tomorrow! You said you'd have lots of research to back this up. I expect to get a copy at lunch today when we meet with that big donor from the casino. What the hell has been wrong with you lately, anyway? Oh, and I know you always check these, Mary. If Newman isn't in yet, have his new guy take over until we can find Newman."

4. Big Chamber of Commerce annual meeting this Thursday night. I've got an email from Mr. Newman that asks me to dig up comparisons between Nosocomial and our cross-town rival, Hope Hospital. I did the digging. I'm

just not sure how heavy we should go on the comparison. We've made great strides against them, but I think it might be a mistake to use numbers to show that we're gaining on those uppities. We hate them, but maybe Mr. Newman should not be "taking the gloves off" and bragging that after 20 years, our numbers and our billings are damn near equal to theirs. Tough call. Until we can find Mr. Newman, I guess you'll have to make that call, Mr. Towershot.

5. CONFIDENTIAL: Mr. Towershot, please read the document I sealed in an envelope and attached to this memo. Cookies told me that as soon as you read it, I must shred and burn it. Will go down to the incinerator in about an hour:

MEMO: HIGHLY CONFIDENTIAL
TO: Newman and the new guy
SUBJECT: Professional Patient

An informant and friend who sometimes works with our state hospital association has notified me that a professional patient has moved into our city. The pro pat does not like Catholic hospitals, so it's likely he will target us instead of those knuckleheads at Hope. The problem, as you likely know, is that some people who have been labeled "professional patients" have sued hospitals and have won major libel settlements. Therefore, from now on, we will refer to such people as "special and immediate needs clients." It is my understanding that this particular special and immediate needs client just got an out-of-court settlement from a Des Moines hospital that ultimately refused to admit and treat him. We can't let that happen. Newman, you're a schmoozer with connections, so ask around to discover what this guy's name is. Everybody I know in Des Moines is tight-lipped on this. Then find a way to do some internal PR so all our medical staff is aware of this guy, but don't leave any kind of trail of communication. You PR guys are supposed to be good at that kind of communicating and cover-up. He could show up at Nosocomial at any time! I don't need the hassle of dealing directly with these hypochondriac nutcases! While you're at it, if you track him down, see if you can't get him to reconsider his stance on Catholic hospitals. Tell him their pharmacy is twice as big as ours and, if necessary, that we're not affiliated with any religion but Hope has God on their side!

6. Mr. Towershot: This is way past due. I suggest you deal with it first. Dr. Sawbones is the chief of our medical staff and carries a lot of clout in the

community. (The running joke is his motto: "Speak softly and carry a big saw." Ha! DuBois might be a backwater town, but we've got some funny folks here, huh?) Sawbones has been after Mr. Newman to feature his photo in our next advertising campaign. Evidently, Mr. Newman featured another doc last month and Sawbones immediately alleged favoritism. I know that Mr. Newman has a photo of Sawbones, but we still need copy to go under his picture. Very flattering copy. Expect to see Sawbones each and every day in this office. Nice guy. But very persistent. (Attached are copies of our recent ads. As you can tell, we feature a doc on staff each month. Our administrator thinks that's very wise. I think it's a waste of money.)

7.   I have been with this office for 14 years, three years longer than Mr. Newman. I need a raise. If medical staff unionizes, they'll get a raise. If they don't, Cookies will give them a raise as a reward for not unionizing. But what about the clerical staff? I've gotten nothing for the past five years! I'm thinking about contacting union organizers myself and lead the push for us 24 clerical/records slaves to get a competitive, decent wage. Also, I am thinking that maybe I might need to take a few weeks' vacation I have built up. Maybe starting tomorrow. I know that puts you in a tough spot. When you see Cookies, please tell him that I am indispensable to you and your transition, particularly since we cannot find Mr. Newman who, in my estimation, finally went bonkers and really is down in New Orleans sipping mimosas. You'll have to take my word on this: You won't survive without me. Get me at least two bucks more an hour.

8. Human Resources reminded me that you must fill out paperwork before noon today if you want to get paid two weeks from today. HR head Wahlert Hempstead is a real **tch. Don't let her get under your skin. She is an Iowa State fanatic. Don't let her bother you when she rants that U of I is a "drug and party school." Which, of course, it is.

9.   I was supposed to have your Responsibility Projections report on Friday to pass on. Actually, it is Mr. Newman's report I need. We fill these out the first of every month. It's supposed to keep all departments in the hospital aware of what the other departments are up to. Thirty big boxes to fill in. I'll email the electronic form. Just fill in any crap. Nobody reads these anyway. I used to do Mr. Newman's for him. Then that HR **tch found out and complained   to

Cookies. So you have to do it. I can't get caught again. I can, however, sit with you in your office and dictate what you might put in those blanks. It should take less than 2 hours. It will only take that long because I will have to tutor you on all the jargon we use around here. Glad to do it.

10. By the way, I am old-fashioned in that I like to lay everything out on paper. Be advised that I will be picking up this memo from you in an hour, shredding it and taking it with the other material to the incinerator. So take notes, but make sure nobody can really decipher those notes. Trust me on this. People at this hospital are such deciphering spies, backstabbers and buttinski busybodies, it's amazing they get any other work accomplished. Come to think of it, some of them don't.

11. We lost a patient. That happens sometimes. I know this because I know all of the intercom codes. And by "lost" I do not mean "died." Physically lost. Did you hear "Code L" earlier this morning? Lost patient. I guess they're still looking for him. I hope it's not that professional patient you are supposed to track down. Many get lost on purpose. We usually find them in Laundry, sucking on some kind of meds they filched from pharmacy. That can get ugly. Cookies usually hides in his office at those times and has Mr. Newman deal with that mess.

12. The newsletter is due at the printers in two days. The online version is already out there. But we haven't made any progress on the print version we mail to 10,000 households. Our printer will charge us an extra fee of $1,000 if we don't stick to the deadline. He's the cheapest in town. But has so much business that his schedules are very tight. Very. By the way, we're already $500 over our printing budget, and it's only June! That ***hole Packer Deere in accounting is worse than that ***ch in HR! He's gonna want answers as to why we're over budget, and he won't care if this is your first day on the job. You are in charge. That's all he cares about: holding a party responsible for fiscal irresponsibility. Any party.

For your consideration:

➤➤ 12-1: Well, it looks like you are "it," at least until they find Newman. Your first order of business will be to prioritize those 12 items your secretary gave you.

➤➤ 12-2: Next: Whether you can afford the time or not, you will need to meet the key personnel that Mary has alluded to in her memo. At lunch, ask the administrator if you can use his name in support of the concessions and extensions you will obviously need to acquire in order to meet those dozen obligations.

➤➤ 12-3: McDonald's is hiring. Few would blame you if you walked out. WWGCD? What would George Costanza do?

➤➤ 12-4: Why didn't your PR courses prepare you for this?

➤➤ 12-5: And what do you intend to do with Mary Richards? Are you taken aback by her rough language and her bluntness? Or, on the other hand, will her candor help get you through this ordeal?

Case 13: And Now for Something Completely Different!

It's Not a Monty Python Skit, Either

You're not too young to remember Monty Python, the movies and the TV programs. In fact, two years after outstanding work and valuable experience at a nonprofit, you, Terry Dupengreedy, 27, are ready to move on. Your goal and rallying cry: *Something completely different* than the 50-hour weeks you spent as a PR assistant at International Organ Donors in Washington, D.C. You want corporate PR. You want the big bucks. And it looks like corporate may, indeed, want you.

This will be your second interview at Fargo Sewers, a Washington D.C. based finance company that lends money to municipalities that need to upgrade or expand their infrastructures. Fargo Sewers provides an alternative to the immediate floating of bond issues. Since many of municipal bond requests must go to the electorate for approval, Fargo Sewers offers politicians an alternative to the high risk that the voters will turn down a request for bonds for essential community improvements, the voters knowing that their taxes will be raised as a result of the bond issue. Evidently, Fargo Sewers likes you as a Counselor of Fund Requests because you had great success in persuading people to donate their organs to those in need. Says Jack Chumpseeker, CEO at Fargo Sewers, as he greets you when you enter his office for the second interview: "You're the PR guy who can talk people out of an arm or a leg or a kidney. You can get the bereaved to donate a loved one's body parts. I like that. Here, we talk people into bypassing the messy voting process and going with Fargo Sewers to maintain their municipal fiscal health yet still fulfill a dream of a better community. In other words, convince people to give something up (an immediate referendum) for the betterment of others. Actually, all we want is a delay in the referendum. You've got the sincere,

I'm-here-to-help-you deportment kind of talent we need at Fargo Sewers. We convince community leaders that there is a legal way to raise money for community improvements that does not involve the nasty 'r' word: 'referendum' and does not rely on the dastardly 't' scare: 'taxes'! And they can do it with very few upfront costs for years! Your boss here will explain."

Your Boss Looks like a Combination of Karl and Groucho

Chumpseeker seems to be talking like you already have the job. He introduces Marx Karloco, a 50-something man with a big smile and a huge mustache. Karloco is V.P. of Fund Requests. "The idea, of course, is to make Fargo Sewers municipal fund requests seem at first to be very difficult to fulfill. Most of the politicians from the 100 medium-sized cities we target in the United States think that getting approval from Fargo Sewers is damn difficult. Like getting a date with a supermodel. And we want to keep that perception intact. By the way Dupengreedy, your competition for this job works for the American Dental Association. We're looking at him because we want our politician clients to think that getting an ILILOBG (Infrastructure Loan in Lieu of Bond Grant) from Fargo Sewers is like "pulling teeth!" Karloco's eyebrows go up and down. You fully expected Chico to come dashing around the corner and in a second, blowing a bicycle horn to punctuate the lame joke. Chumpseeker howls. You decide to howl along with him. Then Karloco asks, "So when can you start?"

You Have Many Questions, But...

"In four weeks."

Actually, you did want clarification on a number of aspects of the job, another new "counselor" position added to Karloco's stable, but something Chumpseeker said immediately after Karloco asked when you could start elicited your favorable response: "Dupengreedy, we pay twice what you are making at the organ donor chop shop. You also get a car and a generous expense account for travel."

"Make that in two weeks," you say.

Training to go out in the Field

Marx Karloco is an excellent mentor. In two weeks you learn everything you need to know about Fargo Sewers, except (which you will learn much later) that they are under investigation by a number of government agencies, including the Consumer Financial Protection Bureau. The major elements of the background you received from Marx:

A. Most of the politicians in the 100 target cities believe that Fargo Sewers is a private contractor for the government and an arm of the Aid to Small Cities Bureau. Marx tells you this "is not exactly true," but that to clarify matters would only undermine the "longstanding credibility" Fargo Sewers has built up. He says there is no need to tell clients that Fargo Sewers is no longer associated with any arm of government.

B. Fargo Sewers does have an impressive pedigree. They started out as part of FDR's public works programs. Their mission was to improve the sanitary conditions in small U.S. cities. They gave grants and low-cost loans to many cities to build or enhance their sewer capabilities. Of course, those cities employed hundreds to make those improvements. "Can you dig it?" Marx quips. You have learned to howl just like Chairman Chumpseeker. The first project was funded for sewers in Fargo, ND, in 1934.

C. In 1960, Chumpseeker's grandfather bought the Fargo Sewers name from the government. Actually, he acquired it for free. Many of FDR's social programs had long since become defunct, so all Chumpseeker's grandfather really had to do was appropriate (steal) the name. Nobody contested him. He went on to build the name and image of Fargo Sewers by offering low-cost grants for many different infrastructure improvements to small cities. These now included bridges, roads and parks, to name a few. Their motto: "FDR IS STILL LOOKING OUT FOR YOU!"

D. Your job (which it turns out also includes generous bonuses for the recruiting of clients) is to go to a target city, get to know the elected leadership and then convince them that a grant from Fargo Sewers will be a much more economical and politically safe way to go instead of the immediate floating of a bond issue. You are impressed that a project a politician would love to have his name on—like the proposed Mayor Weiner Bridge in Syracuse—costs little to finance upfront. In fact, you tell your clients that the first three years of the grant payments could "almost be paid for out of petty cash." In addition, you note, Fargo Sewers will do all the PR for the politician and the winning of a difficult-to-obtain-but-quite-a-coup-when-you-do Fargo Sewers grant. Also, the Fargo Sewers PR arm will be there all three years the grant is in operation, building grass-roots support for the conversion of the grant to a bond issue.

E. By the way, as soon as you meet your quota of getting four municipalities to apply for a grant, you have been promised a promotion to Director of Public Relations for the Fargo Sewers Midwest Division. So you have to pay your dues in the sales area, and that learning will result in full-time PR campaigning in Midwestern communities that have received grants.

You Are Very Good at What You Do

Within two years, you have recruited seven city leaders to apply for grants. True to his word, Chairman Chumpseeker promotes you to PR Director-Midwest and you begin to design campaigns to convince local voters in those seven municipalities that the very low-cost "seed grants" should eventually be converted into bond issues that Fargo Sewers will "underwrite." You love your job. Well, that is until the subpoena…

For your consideration:
(all from the Joint Congressional Committee on Municipal Investment Fraud; you are now sitting before that committee)

➡ 13-1: Mr. Dupengreedy, were you not aware that your company paid you those lucrative bonuses because you brought in politicians who, in turn, took bribes in the form of so-called grants?

➧ 13-2: Mr. Dupengreedy, are you aware that Fargo Sewers charged hundreds of departments in various municipalities fees for service but never got their consent to actually do so?

➧ 13-3: Mr. Dupengreedy, do you really think that Fargo Sewers could finance a bridge repair project for payments of $500 a month from municipalities over three years without losing money?

➧ 13-4: Mr. Dupengreedy, do you know the differences between "grants," "loans" and "bribes"?

➧ 13-5: Mr. Dupengreedy, as Midwest head of PR for Fargo Sewers, were you really so naïve as to think that after three years the voters were not being bilked by passing a referendum to float a bond to pay Fargo Sewers for the next 17 years? And are you not aware that Fargo Sewers gets an average of 15 percent annually when the bond issue passes? Fifteen percent for providing a three-year, low cost "grant"? Wouldn't you like to own bonds with that kind of yield?

➧ 13-6: Mr. Dupengreedy, what did your boss Chairman Chumpseeker know, and when did he know it? When did you allegedly confer with him and tell him "there's a cancer growing on your chairmanship"?

➧ 13-7: Mr. Dupengreedy, your only defense for overlooking what you call "improprieties" is what you call "blind ambition"? Are all PR people like you? Have you ever heard of the reprehensible marketing ploy known as 'bait and switch'?

Case 14: Your Own Agency upon Graduation? No Way!

Way!

They don't recommend it. After all, students graduate with a degree in PR and most of them yearn for an entry-level job under the tutelage of a seasoned professional. Regular hours. Regular paycheck. You, Walenda Highwire, graduate from SUNY Millard Fillmore and decide to "go it alone" and start your own PR agency immediately out of college. Of course, the first year of agency existence you were ensconced in your parents' basement in suburban Buffalo. Yes, very low overhead—and that was good because you started out as a volunteer PR practitioner for several nonprofits. But that built up the portfolio quickly. You positioned yourself as being "a top-quality, inexpensive alternative" to established PR agencies. Soon you had your first paying client. Of course, it didn't hurt that your social media skills were decidedly better than those of nearly anyone employed by the local agencies. Word got around quickly. In just over a year, you were ready to move out of the basement, hire a secretary and open an office. Way to go, Walenda! You certainly beat the odds.

What next? Should you hire an entry-level PR person instead of a secretary? Would your professor and mentor at Fillmore approve of your idea that the new hire could be part secretary and part PR practitioner? You thought not.

Your Mentor Weighs In

You sit down to lunch with Evetta Lee, professor extraordinaire. And you are buying. You are surprised to hear her advice: that if you can share some secretarial duties with your new hire, it might make sense to hire a recent Fillmore PR grad. Dr. Lee reminds you that an entry-level PR person wants the valuable experience that comes with the first job. Just make sure you give your new hire responsibilities that go beyond answering phones and updating mailing lists. Delegate wisely. Add more responsibilities as the new hire grows professionally. "Delegate the good stuff and that hire won't mind sharing the mundane tasks, too." In fact, Dr. Lee has what she believes is a strong candidate for your job. This candidate entered the PR program after you graduated, having only PR courses remaining to earn her degree. "She's bright, hard-working and flexible in what tasks she will take on," Dr. Lee tells you. "Of course, knowing you, Walenda, I'm not sure she can keep up with your 14-hour days seven days a week. Do you have any kind of life outside of your agency duties?"

No, Not Really. No Life to Speak of. Not Currently.

The past year, you have lived and breathed Walenda Communications. You believe that is the cost of being an underdog upstart. No social life, apart from schmoozing clients. No time to even do pilates, which you loved doing as an undergrad. All business all the time. You wonder if it is possible that your obsession could actually set a bad example for Dyna Moe, Dr. Lee's choice for your new employee. Might Dyna want a boss who has a well-rounded life? Might Dyna draw the line at working nights and weekends? I guess you'd discover that during the interview.

Amazing. Someone on the planet who was as much of a workaholic as Walenda Highwire? Impossible! The first month on the job, Dyna mostly slept at her desk. She brought in three new client accounts and never complained about any of the secretarial tasks she was asked to do. Her writing was excellent. She had videography skills that saved your agency a lot of money, as you did not need to outsource video projects. And she never seemed tired. She always dressed professionally. She could be opinionated when it came to the development of strategy and tactics for clients, but she always remained a team player, offering candid insights and then ultimately relying on your judgment. If Dyna ever did complain about your management style, you never heard about it. Of course, the only one likely to tell you anything about Dyna's discontent, if there was any, would be her cat. Apart from taking care of the cat, Dyna had no other life, either.

It's the Fourth Year Already

Things went so well that as your agency started its fourth year, you were considering hiring yet another employee. Dyna liked the idea. She had been with you now for two years: "There are several Fillmore students graduating this year who Dr. Lee says would be great additions to your staff," she says. "I'd be glad to help recruit and train them." You remind Dyna that you can only afford *one* new hire. Then she drops the bombshell: "Well, I've had a great experience here," she says, "but I think it's time I went out on my own. So you'd need to replace me, too."

You should have anticipated that. Dyna was also the kind who could have succeeded starting her own agency in Buffalo right out of college. Now, after two years with you, she did plan to start her own agency. Is there any way you can dissuade her from doing so? Give her a raise? Give her an equal partnership? Highwire-Moe Communications. Maybe that would work?

Flattered but Needs to Move on

"You've worked your butt off for this agency, Dyna. Now it's time to reap the rewards. A full partnership. Let's grow together!"

"I'm flattered. And I've learned so much from you, Walenda. But I'll always feel like the back-up quarterback. I need to run my own team. Understand?"

"Of course, I do. And I wish you the best of success. But just curious: Could I have done anything better as a manager? What are your complaints? I really want to know."

"No complaints."

"Any suggestions for improvement?"

"None."

"Are you sure? Maybe I should have a candid talk with your cat instead…"

For your consideration:

▶▶ 14-1: Why do people wish others good luck when those others are competing against them? They really DO NOT want any kind of good luck that would enhance the competition's chances of winning the game and leave them big losers. Dyna took four of your top nine clients with her. Then, to make matters worse, after you trained her talented replacement (who, because of budget constraints, could only be hired at three-quarter time with no benefits), Dyna offered her a full-time position and the replacement went over to Dyna's shop. It wasn't as hard to hate somebody you once admired as you thought it might be. Should you run the risk of alienating Dyna by confronting her with the fact that she had no complaints and no suggestions for improvement, yet she, in your opinion, then stabbed you in the back?

▶▶ 14-2: You go see Dr. Lee. What advice should you now solicit from your mentor? You have heard through the grapevine that one of the clients Dyna stole is unhappy with Dyna's work. Is it right to try to woo that client back?

▶▶ 14-3: You now have a social life. You now have a boyfriend. And a dog. You have season tickets to Buffalo Bills games. You do pilates regularly. You no longer spend 14-hour days on the job. In fact, you are almost content with being a one-person shop again, but a shop with fewer clients. You make a passable (but no longer great) income. You used to make fun of folks who "got too contented." Does this "new you" scare you?

Some public relations programs at colleges and universities offer dynamic learning environments with mentoring professors who are constantly available for consultation. Other programs don't seem all that eager to help undergrads become successful entry-level practitioners. Toby Truthseeker finally found the right department. They prepared him well to lead the student-run marcom agency as a senior, a joint project of the Marketing, PR and Advertising departments. In fact, a local bank has asked Truthseeker's agency to help with the planning of a campaign. The problem: What the affable bank president has already done for the campaign is...gulp!...awful.

Case 15: Be Honest or be Praised and Eligible for a Possible Job? May I have Both?

The Catalyst for Your Transfer

You now know it was a good idea to transfer from Peoria University to Rockford Tech. As a second-semester sophomore at P.U., you, Toby Truthseeker, joined the PRSSA group and soon discovered what a terrible chapter P.U. had. Essentially, the group met (irregularly) and ate pizza. Sure, they talked about what projects and fund-raisers they would like to do, but nobody ever got around to doing anything. Both the president and vice-president of P.U. PRSSA were what your father calls "slackers." Clearly, all either of them wanted was that leadership designation on their resumes. Evidently, this was not the first year that P.U. PRSSA did virtually nothing. Last year, when their dynamic leader, Jo Biden-Sanders, became a delegate and governing board member for national PRSSA, she stopped doing anything for her local chapter. Although the Communications Department at P.U. got plenty of favorable buzz on-campus because of Jo's accomplishment at the national level, as soon as Jo left, PRSSA became a joke. However, it was a carefully guarded inside joke, and it seemed like only you fully recognized how bad that chapter was. So you went to have a conversation with the chapter's faculty adviser.

Actually, you dropped in during the adviser's office hours. But a note on the door said she couldn't keep her office hours that day. So you went the next day. Same note. Finally, you tracked down PRSSA adviser Barbara Poultice when you heard there was a departmental faculty meeting. You waited outside until the meeting was over. Then you asked Dr. Poultice if you could make an appointment. She was polite, but noted that it would be about a week before she could fit you in. Then she put it in her datebook calendar.

One Week Later...

So a week went by. You went to your appointment. Poultice must have forgotten about it. Or maybe she had something better to do. You thought that maybe you could catch her at the next PRSSA meeting, but the vice president of PRSSA told you that "she never shows up. She trusts us to take care of matters. She's real busy with other stuff."

"Well, maybe if she spent more time with the chapter, we could get moving on some worthwhile projects," you tell a fellow PRSSA member, Buzz Backpatter. He laughs.

"She's still basking in the glory of getting a P.U. PR student on national board," Buzz says. "And I'm not even sure Poultice even knows that B.S. (Biden-Sanders) has nothing to do with our local chapter anymore. B.S. thinks it's beneath her now. If you ask me, I think Poultice thinks the whole adviser thing is beneath her, too. Me, I'm transferring to Rockford Tech. I hear they've got a PRSSA chapter that kicks butt!"

"But I hear the PR courses here at P.U. are pretty good," you say.

"Maybe they used to be. Poultice has the Principles class. I was in it last semester. She probably showed up half the time. But who the hell would complain? I've talked to a lot of students who were in there with me. Nobody I talked to got below an "A." Poultice is working this semester on some kind of PR project for the provost. Nobody sees her much. But I don't know how I'm going to do in the upcoming Cases class here with Dr. Rosethorn. I hear he's tough. I think I'm going to audit Principles again when I get to Rockford."

"Wait for me, Buzz! I'm coming, too!"

Off to Rockford

What a difference Rockford made! Their PRSSA chapter had no national governing board student celebrities, but it did have an ambitious local governing board of four hard-working students. They also had an involved faculty adviser. During the fall, they already had a written draft of a plan for their Bateman Competition entry. Furthermore, they sponsored a student-run PR agency that actually had more than a dozen community clients from the Rockford and Chicago exurbs area. "We have to be careful this year," said the agency head, Quitea Catch. "A few Chicago-area agencies have half-jokingly complained that we're stealing their potential clients!"

A year later, your senior year, you are elected head of Marcom Rockford, the agency that takes pride in its work and its client list. Life is good and not all that complex. Well, good and relatively simple until Prairie Bank came calling.

An Affable Guy with an Awful Approach

Titus Vault had heard good things about Marcom Rockford. In fact, he called you and asked if you and your agency crew could visit his bank. Marcom Rockford had never had a bank client before, so you were excited to take Mr. Vault up on his invitation. Nice, friendly guy. And his reputation as a knowledgeable banker was legend.

"We're not quite big enough yet to enlist one of those fancy marcom agencies in Chicago," he tells you and two cohorts as you sit in the Prairie Bank board room and chomp on donuts. "But we can pay you Rockford students a decent honorarium if you'd look over the campaign that I and my head cashier have developed." He has copies for all three of you. "We've been working on this for more than a year now and, frankly, we're pretty dang proud of it. Forty pages total, with 15 alone devoted to our bank history. Give it a look-see and make some suggestions, if any are needed. Also, I should tell you that when we launch this campaign, we'll be likely buying at least one bank—probably more—in the Belvidere area. I'd sure like one of you soon-to-graduate Rockford students to get in on the ground floor of all this expansion and carry through with the plan. I sure would! We'd want to hire our first PR rep. Maybe you, Mr. Truthseeker! I hear good things about you."

Attached (exhibits 15-A and 15-B) are a few parts of the plan that Vault wants to implement. Although he exhorts you to "be honest," you do wonder if you can do that (you KNOW that the client deserves your honesty above all) and yet still have a shot at that PR rep job that looks so very inviting. Hmm…Vault has outstanding credentials as a banker. But as a PR strategist…Hmm…

"Oh, and one more thing: Doctor Poultice-Geist at P.U.—yeah, she used to be married—got a copy of this document. She and I go way back. We went to Freeport High together: go Pretzels! I asked her to run the campaign by her PR kids and give it a look-see herself. Finally got a nice, brief note from her and her crew: short but sweet: "It all looks good. Go for it, Titus!"

For your consideration:

▸▸ 15-1: How does the sample news release stack up against others you have seen? Critique it. (Exhibit 15-A)

▸▸ 15-2: You know that the best objectives are those that are quantitative and deadline-oriented. How would you characterize Prairie Bank's sample objective?

▸▸ 15-3: Naturally, research is an important element of a PR plan. Evidently, Mr. Vault saved money and did the research himself. Do you suggest more research? Different research? If so, HOW will you suggest it to Mr. Vault?

▸▸ 15-4: In sum, how does the Prairie Bank campaign document compare to what you learned about planning in your PR Campaigns class?

▸▸ 15-5: You have scheduled a meeting with Mr. Vault to go over your plan critique. What do you tell him?

<u>Exhibit 15-A:</u>

News! News! News! News!

From your friends at Prairie Bank!

**<u>For publication in the Rockford Register, Chicago Tribune and other fine
media and for immediate release: (date here)</u>**

Contact: Mr. Vault at 000-123-45678

Prairie Announces Realignment of Personnel Components!

Titus T. Vault, CPA and President of Prairie Bank Holdings Ltd., announces the
realignment of personnel components, as Edna C. Greenback has been promoted to
head cashier at Prairie Bank, Rockford, up from the teller line. This makes room for the
advancement of Clearance K. Flapdoodle from Rockford cashier to V.P. of operations at
Prairie's new Belvidere Branch (add address when we know it).

"I am pleased as punch to open another branch of our very-successful, client-
centered bank operation," said Mr. Vault. "We are going to offer the same great
personal attention at Belvidere that we do at Prairie Rockford. I and Mr. Flapdoodle, a
Belvidere High grad (go Buzzards!) guarantee it."

To celebrate the Prairie expansion, Mr. Vault has deemed next week as Toaster
Tuesday. Open a Rockford Free Checking account at the new Belvidere branch and
get a free toaster!

"And just to make things more down-home friendly and interesting, my wife Vera
is going to bake up some loaves of her famous poppyseed rye homemade bread and
give out fresh slices to the first 50 folks who qualify for a toaster!" Mr. Vault gushes with
Prairie pride.

Even though we are expanding, Prairie has no intention of being a big-city bank.

"Face it: the closer you get to Chicago, the more frigging impersonal banks seem
to be. That WILL NEVER be the case with Prairie and our sister banks. No way! Said
Mr. Vault."

Prairie has been a Rockford Chamber of Commerce "Rock Solid" award winner
for five straight years and is a member of the FDIC.   -30-

Exhibit 15-B:
(Some excerpts from the Prairie PR plan)

OBJECTIVE:
To make people feel welcome.

TACTIC:
To give away toasters. *(This is just one sample tactic.)*

STRATEGY:
We position ourselves against the impersonal banks (all of them) in Chicago. *(The plan goes on for five pages on Vault's definition of "impersonal" with various anecdotes from his 30 years as a personal banker.)*

GOAL:
Increase our holdings and net worth but not seem uppity.

PUBLIC RELATIONS MEDIA:
Get the big Chicago newspapers to do feature stories on us. If we need to buy some ad space to get that consideration, that's OK. We have budgeted for that. Also, Mr. Vault will want to toot on Tooter. In addition, maybe do an ad with the NTA, National Toaster Association. They can share the cost. Also, news releases at least once a week. Important things happen at Prairie Bank that never seem to get run. We'll get a PR rep to get the coverage we deserve. And if the poppyseed bread idea takes off, Vera can bake more.

RESEARCH:
Mr. Vault conducted a **focus group** of his bank employees. They all think this expansion and PR venture is a great idea. They think the toasters giveaway is a great idea. They think that the poppyseed bread idea is the greatest idea. And they like the fact that we're going to take a shot at impersonal Chicago banking.
Survey: Prairie Bank customers were surveyed as they left the bank. Here are a few questions and the results:

A. Why is Prairie your favorite bank? (102 responses, and all positive) Example: "The donuts." Example: "Titus takes time with me." Example: "I hate Chicago banks." Example: "My great grandpa banked here. He got most of his money back during the Grate Depression."

B. It's time that Prairie spread its goodwill and native charm to Belvidere and maybe beyond: 67 Strongly Agree; 23 Agree; 2 Unsure

C. How would you characterize Prairie's personal service. (circle just one) GREAT. SUPER. STUPENDOUS (34 GREAT; 57 SUPER and 11 STUPENDOUS)

D. WHAT would you *improve* about Prairie Bank? Nothing! (101) "Get more cream-filled donuts. You always seem to run out by the time I do my banking. I don't like plain. (1)

Case 16: Dickie Fleegle's Cow Patty Bingo Crisis

Dickie Dumps a Load of Grief on His Best Friend

Another sleepless night, Charlie. Thanks for reading my emails. This is likely to be a long, rambling one. Sorry about that. I should have gone to grad school with you two years ago rather than take this PR job in Madison. Silly, stupid me. You are now on the verge of a master's—and I'm on the verge of a nervous breakdown. And like you, I earned it.

Remember when we graduated and I boasted that working for the Madison Area All Faiths Coalition would save my godless soul? And you said, "Hey, if there really were a god, would he be so cruel as to give a guy with your talent 150 bucks a week and no benefits? That's downright satanic!" Every time I remember that remark I laugh. And laughter is so good for me these days. I need more laughter. But I don't think I'll regain my sense of humor by staying in Madison. Need a roommate for the fall?

I hate to bother you with this again, but I clearly am having a crisis of faith. Remember Doc Flackstermeister used to tell us that "PR can grow to have a better reputation than it does now. When you start out in the field, just have faith. Oh, and also a thick skin and a second job at Burger Barn!" I love that guy. Great sense of humor and a realist we all wanted to emulate. If he had not died so young, I'd be sending some of these long, whining emails to him, asking for advice. Of course, I can almost predict what his advice would be: "Scheisskopf, (ed. note: Dickie's nickname from a favorite book: *Catch-22*) quit feeling sorry for yourself. You picked a nonprofit. You want to make positive change in this mixed-up world. You chose a profession that some people think is one that encourages manipulation and lying. But it could be much worse. You could have got an accounting or a law degree! Ha!" To use a bad pun, here is an "account" of what has happened so far, legally and otherwise.

The good: In the past 22 months, I have made or exceeded my fund-raising goal each month. The deal when I talked myself into creating this PR job was that I would raise twice my salary each month, thereby deflecting that age-old mandate that many PR people face: Prove your worth!

More good: The All Faiths food bank was full for the first time ever last month. The fund for building the new homeless shelter is growing. Favorable media coverage for All Faiths has quadrupled since I took over. Our Web site now looks much better, and we get a hell of a lot more hits. OK, I brag a bit. And why not? I not only sold the All Faiths Board on the new position, but I came through with my promises.

The bad: Charlie, I am beginning to believe the worst about people. In fact, I think the churched are among the worst! Such bickering at board meetings! I swear I almost had to intervene to break up a potential fist fight between a Mennonite and a Quaker. I kid you not! Turf wars. Petty ideological differences. I thought all that nonsense was above and beyond those who lead the charge to sacredness, sanctity and all that other "stuff." Sorry, maybe some sleep would help me regain my perspective.

More bad: Last weekend. Another creative fund-raiser on my part. I brag again. And why not? We raised nearly FIVE GRAND simply by marking off a field and getting a cow to crap in that field. FIVE GRAND! But here's what wasn't grand about Cow Patty Bingo: All the crap ultimately landed on me. Just because I like to add a bit of humor to what I do. Some little kid got all scared, started crying and pointing at me. Then it really hit the fan: His mom: "That's cruel. If Sammy says you hit the cow hard on the head with that hammer, then you hit the cow hard on the head with that hammer! My child does not lie. Your board and PETA are definitely going to hear from me, Sonny."

"Sonny"????? OK, all the sectors of the pasture had been sold and cordoned off. People waited patiently for the winning plop. And waited. Many came and went. But 'ol Bessie wouldn't do her business. Four hours of wandering inside the fenced area in those chalked-off and marked-off sectors and not so much as a fart. I kid you not! Of course, I had my hammer and went around pounding back in the stakes that contained the names of the donors who bought each plot for potential plopping and the winning of the $1,000 first prize. Bessie knocked over quite a few. I ran around like a rodeo clown, pounding stakes and shouting encouragement to Bessie to get the job done. I guess I got a little carried away, trying to show my mock "frustration" regarding an outcome that still had not come out in over four hours. So I made some FAKE hammer blows to Bessie's head. FAKE ones. Some of the crowd around the fence laughed. I guess it did look pretty real. And that one kid got scared. "Sonny" the clown ran over and I tried to explain to the mom. Too late. Now it's me who is in deep "stuff."

OK, enough rambling. Some anxiety relieved. I'm going to try to go to sleep again. My boss told me yesterday that he was "against having PR stunts from the start." He says he believes I actually hit that cow on the head! Hard. And he says even if I did not, "the perception is the reality." I do have to agree. It seems like all of Madison has turned against me. Big photo on the front page of the Madison Courier! Me running around like a clown on all the TV news programs. Thankfully, nobody caught my FAKE hammering of Bessie's head on camera. Charlie, I LOVE COWS. Hell, I'm a vegetarian! And Madison? The town of the liberal, the forgiving, the givers of the benefit of the doubt? Those hypocrites! I am so ashamed of Madison! I expected better. Much better. And that kid crying on TV-7 Action News. They keep running the same crying jag during each, updated daily story. And they got hold of the guy who supposedly "invented" Cow Patty Bingo and supposedly owns the rights to the phrase itself. But HIS phrase is Cow *PIE* Bingo! He's suing me and All Faiths! Holy mierda! So to speak.

End of diatribe. This time for sure I stop the rambling. I miss you, Charlie. Will call you this weekend. You were a great roommate. Oh, and that's the other thing. BOTH my roommates moved out. They said all the media attention was driving them crazy and that they really didn't want to be associated with a guy who beats on cows. I won't have enough for next month's rent if I'm living here alone. But, actually, that's the least of my concerns right now. See ya –Dickie.

For your consideration:

➡ 16-1: It's good to have somebody to vent to. At this time, does Dickie need to seek out more help and counseling than his former roommate can provide?

16-2: Give Dickie credit for wanting to do good in the world and taking the initiative to advocate for and start a PR program that, except for the Cow Patty Bingo misunderstanding, is largely successful. Had you known that something like this would explode, would you have, in retrospect, Dickie, still tried to create that job?

16-3: Most students study crisis communications by examining the big cases. Exxon Valdez. Tylenol tampering. Three-Mile Island. Dominos on YouTube. BP Gulf oil spill. And dozens more. It is highly unlikely that "Dickie 'The Hammer' Fleegle and Constipated Bessie Do Cow Patty Bingo' will ever make that list. But it still is a bona fide crisis. Given your knowledge in how to proceed in a crisis, what advice do you have for Dickie? What advice do you have for the All Faiths Board of Directors?

16-4: What about legal counsel? All Faiths has a crack Madison lawyer and born-again Christian who does a lot of pro bono work for them. Dickie has nobody. Is it time he got a lawyer?

16-5: Isn't Cow Patty Bingo something that cannot be copyrighted? An idea? Dickie sure doesn't need a lawsuit on his hands right now. He has been asked to do an interview with a local TV station regarding the impending suit. How should Dickie handle this? Can he somehow use his media relations knowledge to effectively address this crisis?

16-6: Is this a mess that could never really be completely cleaned up? Dickie was probably kidding, but he did tell Charlie on the phone the next weekend that his "only recourse" seemed to be to "change my identity, leave town and hide somewhere very far away."

➤➤ 16-7: In retrospect, Dickie says he wishes he had immediately called in a veterinarian to examine the cow. But he did not want to incur the expense and he thought the whole thing would blow over in a few days. Now, a vet he consulted says he would be happy to examine Bessie, but over a week's time, cows heal quickly." Ouch.

➤➤ 16-8: It seems that each day brings a new angle on the story. The lawsuit. An initiative on the part of some All Faiths donors to ask for their money back! A swarm of PETA people descending on Madison. Is there any way to stop the media frenzy?

Case 17: You got Older Fast. But did you get Wiser, Hawk?

You Get Promoted to V.P.

It happens quickly. One day you shine bright as a star intern. They are so impressed they hire you after graduation. Two years later: promotion from PR assistant to coordinator. Two more years later: promotion from coordinator to director. You are now in your tenth year at St. Louis Strategists (SLS), one of the largest marcom firms in town. Your V.P. has left to join a prestigious New York City firm. They want you to take over his duties. In effect, you will now run the entire operation, as the agency's president and founder is semi-retired and only comes in once a week, largely just to check his mail, take a nap at his desk and tell "war stories" to anyone who will listen.

What will you do as V.P.? All of your time will be spent in a supervisory capacity. Three creative people will report directly to you. Four department directors, one of them in charge of eight client representatives, will report to you. Two of six support personnel will report to you. And, clearly, all are looking forward to that. It's not that they did not like your predecessor, but they all enjoy and respect your management style over his cautious and conservative style. Your rallying cry has always been: "Do such outstanding work that nobody can question your fun!" They have nicknamed you "Hawkeye," after Hawkeye Pierce of M.A.S.H. fame, the doctor who was so brilliant and so dedicated that his sometimes bizarre antics were always overlooked. These workers do consider you indispensable. They all work hard but also have fun. And it feels good that they like your style. Very good.

Pass on Your Style: Take Interns.

One of your directors, Denny Eagerpleaser, advises you to take interns for supervision: "Hawk, give them an education they will never forget." Little did you know at the time how unforgettable your first intern's education would turn out to be.

Such a practice to take on an intern by top management has never been the case at SLS. SLS does have an intern each semester, but all have been under the supervision of the four department heads, not the V.P. You think back to your own internship experience. Obviously, you performed well—so well that they hired you at SLS. Indeed, your supervisor, a director of creatives, was an excellent mentor. But how much better could your experience have been had you gotten at least some wisdom and direction from the corner office? Yes, it's time to give back. You do decide to devote some quality time to the next intern. In fact, the more you think about it, the more you look forward to it.

The Spoof is Set

What might be the best way to introduce the new intern to the unique SLS culture under your leadership? What about an innocuous practical joke? Yes, you believe such an approach will allow her to see that marketing communication can be fun, that people work hard but that they enjoy their jobs and their colleagues. You certainly would have appreciated the joking attention to ease your tension your first day on the internship front. You were slightly scared and intimidated. Humor is a wonderful ice-breaker. But what to do? It has been only 10 years since you were an ambitious neophyte ready to enter the PR world. College could not have changed all that much since you were there. You all appreciated people who had senses of humor. Your best professors were those who were lively and engaging, sticklers for performance, but also occasional entertainers. Yes, a welcoming joke is in order. That kind of thing never goes out of style. Right?

At the end of their regular weekly meeting, the entire staff is all smiles as they discuss a way to welcome the new intern. Your creative director suggests that since the intern has never met V.P. Hawkeye before, that he actually become Hawkeye Pierce. One of your very talented secretaries, who for years you have been trying to convert to a writer's position (but she doesn't want the unconventional hours and extra responsibility) says that you look "much more like The Dude than Hawkeye." In fact, she volunteers to help you with the wig and the beard. Most in attendance know immediately that she is referring to the main character in the now cult-classic film "The Big Lebowski." Before long a chant goes up in the meeting: "The Dude Abides! The Dude Abides!" That settles it.

The Intern Meets The Dude

You agree to secretly videotape the meeting in your office, as the staff wants to see what transpires. All agree that perhaps the intern will fall down with laughter, particularly if she has seen the movie. "Even if she hasn't seen the movie," you note, "she sure has heard about Hippie holdovers, and she'd never expect such a Dude running a serious business operation. I'm sure she'll have fun!"

On the appointed day, Denny ushers Sondra Whisp, 22, into The Dude's office. "Sondra, I want you to meet the incomparable, fearless leader we call The Dude…"

"Oh, shut the hell up, Denny!" you say, avoiding the "f" word on purpose. "You're out of your element, Denny. Get outta here so I can give Ms. Whisp a proper orientation." Then you pretend to suck on a roach clip and hold smoke in your lungs. "Care for a white Russian?" you ask.

"Is that an alcoholic beverage?" she says, not smiling but backing away from your desk. "Imbibing on the job?"

"Yeah. I need one about now. A guy with the same name as me wants me to deliver a million bucks in ransom to his wife's kidnappers. So The Dude can't stay long today. What do you want to know about this marcom operation? Oh, but don't walk over near my bookcase. One of our staff came in here and had an accident on the rug…"

"That's disgusting!" she says. Then she runs out of the office. Before anyone can stop her, she is gone.

A Frantic Call to Her Adviser

Professor Hugh G. Ego at Big Arch State is a good friend. At least once a semester you come to talk to his PR classes. You explain the situation to him. He is

Ms. Whisp's internship academic supervisor. You apologize and say you hope Ms. Whisp sees the welcoming "event" as a joke. You implore him to send her back to work tomorrow so you can give her a proper orientation. Ego is quite amused.

"I'm sure we can work things out. Sondra is one student I don't really know very well. Quiet. Respectful. I know that much. I'll straighten things out with her. And congratulations on the promotion. I presume that big raise will mean a big contribution for the new computer lab in the Big Arch Communication Department?"

"Just fix it so our intern understands me and you'll have that long-overdue big check in the mail tomorrow, Hugh. Count on it."

Are We Good?

Sondra does come back the next day. Hawkeye invites her into his office; this time he is clean-shaven and dressed in a suit. He asks if she talked to her adviser at Arch. She says, "Yes, so I understand now." Wanting to make amends, Hawkeye shows Sondra to her office, an office that yesterday was a messy storage place. There, with a pink bow on it, is a DVD copy of "The Big Lebowski." "I need to go out of town this afternoon," he tells her. "But I've got an important first assignment for you: Here is the file on that mixed martial arts Amateur Iron Man/Woman special scheduled for the St. Louis arena next month. I want you to write it. Then give it to Denny. He'll go over the edits and get it out to the media. This will look great in your portfolio, Sondra. Welcome!"

Not too many interns in their first week get to write a news release. Hawkeye feels like he's done an excellent job in making amends. Sondra smiles and seems eager to get to work. In addition, Hawkeye has erased the tape of his first encounter with Sondra and had a special meeting with employees early in the morning —before Sondra came back— and told all employees never to mention anything about the failed practical joke.

Whimsical Willie Had the Morning Off

Writer Willie Wookiewanka took most of the morning off to go to his daughter's pre-school drama presentation where she played a silent deciduous tree that did, however, rustle her leaves. So he missed the early meeting. He strolled in about 11:30 and, a bit on the boisterous by his very nature, said, "Hey, somebody's got a great little office where there used to be loads of useless crap. Welcome, intern! Did they show your video yet?"

This upset Sondra. "What video?"

"The one where you got punked! Damn, I love John Goodman and that Bridges guy in that movie. How about you?"

Denny Rushes in

"Never mind about that, Willie, Sondra's under deadline with a news release. Just let her do her job in peace."

"Geeze, Denny, she must be very special. I was on staff here as a full-timer for more than a year before you let me do a release! And I had to SHARE an office my first year! Geeze!"

Denny Does His Critique and then Calls Hawkeye at the Airport

"Dammit, Hawk, that kid is sensitive! I marked it up in red a little bit. I thought I was careful not to trash what obviously is a release that needs major work. I thought I made some constructive comments…yeah, she walked out again. But before she walked out, she asked me to give her a different client to work for, as she believes that the bouts we're promoting are "legally sanctioned entertainment to encourage permanent brain damage." **The next day**

Headline in the Archway News, the campus newspaper: *Intern at Local Marcom Firm Alleges "Hostile Work Environment"*

For your consideration (so please abide):

➤ 17-1: Well, you have 10 years' experience, V.P. Hawkeye. Don't you think you should have done some research on the temperament of your intern BEFORE you played the joke? At least have called her academic adviser ahead of time, even if he knew little about her?

➤ 17-2: The campus environment has changed in 10 years, Hawkeye. In fact, had somebody done his/her homework, you would have discovered that Sondra and several other students had earlier in the year filed a grievance against an art professor for making "disturbing comments about the human body" in class. You could never imagine that kind of complaint happening when you were in college. Welcome to the new world of higher education.

➤ 17-3: Is it time to cancel that trip and get back to the office for more damage control?

➤ 17-4: Is it advisable that you, Hawkeye, should make another attempt at reconciliation with Ms. Whisp? At this point, what are your options?

Suddenly you reach middle age. Suddenly you wonder what is wrong with wanting MORE. Is there really a major difference between the life-long journalist and the journalist who eventually goes over to "the dark side"? Yes, the dark side is what some fellow journalists say is the evil place reserved for a reporter or editor who "goes corporate." You went corporate. And now? Maybe you ought to reap the benefits of going even MORE corporate? Your call.

Case 18: 35 and Spin Doesn't Seem so Dizzying Anymore... and a Tie is not Necessarily a Noose

Up from Editor to Publisher

As an undergrad print journalism major, you used to laugh at all your peers who would major in broadcasting and dress up to take their turns as news anchors on the weekly student-run broadcast. Few would ever get to anchor professionally. You called them "perky, pea-brained news readers." They were not real journalists. You also used to laugh at those PR majors who got dressed up and went out to meet clients for their student-run agency. And the advertising majors? They were the ones who couldn't write. They were the ones who watched and critiqued the Super Bowl ads and suddenly considered themselves marketing communicators. Ha!

Back in your time, your major was now underpopulated (and it still is) but, by golly, you were real journalists who didn't have to back a cause or read somebody else's dumbed-down words from a teleprompter to get a paycheck. Free speech and a free press were your cause. Fairness, completeness and objectivity were your solid values. Sure, your first job at a weekly newspaper paid poorly. In fact, your second job two years later at a daily didn't pay all that much better. But your integrity was still intact. You were the one who reported on those who would undermine communities with their drug dealing, their political scheming and their various greedy enterprises. In fact, one of your fellow college Communications majors whose sequence was advertising was now in jail for defrauding clients. You covered the story. Ha! Sometimes there is justice in the world. Besides, you seldom ever had to wear a tie to work, something that in college, and many years after, you considered "a noose."

You are now 35, Pedro Panza Quixote. After working your way up to editor of a five-day-a-week newspaper in a suburb of Indianapolis, a position you have held for three years, the publisher job becomes available. You apply. You get it. You do it for a year. Then you assess what you have done and where you might be headed.

For one, you got a 25 percent bump in salary. True, you no longer write for the paper or supervise talented, young writers, but you don't miss that nearly as much as you thought you would. In fact, most of your time is spent with the advertising sales people and your paper's accountant. Fortunately, your paper circulates in a county with an older population, and many of them still want their newspaper five days a week. Although circulation has not gone up, it has not gone down, either. Of course, some advertisers have dropped your newspaper from their publications priority lists because as your readers get older, their disposable incomes go down. No need for the local sports car dealership to advertise with you anymore. Their primary prospects go elsewhere for their news.

News? Is that what they call it these days? It sure was different 13 years ago when you first started. What are you saying? Now it is YOU, Mr. Publisher, who asks to see the stories to be covered each day. "I'm not trying to influence what you do," you say to the editor who replaced you, a real go-getter who knows how to manage reporters. All I am saying is to look for stories that appeal to our readership and to their consumption habits. And, yes, we're short-staffed, so I do want your reporters to write features for each of our monthly special issue-inserts. Next month: cars. Maybe that sports car dealership doesn't realize that our readers still have a bit of vibrant youth left in them. Check out story opportunities like that. We can't print great journalism unless we get revenue from great print great ads."

What Happened to You?

What happened is that the county's biggest employer, a computer software developer that has grown big and rich and now successfully reaches dozens of overseas markets, is looking for a marketing communications vice president. You know so because their V.P. of Operations sits next to you at Rotary meetings.

"Been looking a little haggard since you got to be publisher, Panzy (your nickname)? Is the text of the First Amendment you had tattooed across your heart fading a bit? A third baby on the way? Is life not exactly as black and white as you once thought it was? Join us. And I'm not kidding. That publisher salary you make? Our international travel budget for you would amount to more than that."

You are surprised when you utter the following. "I'll think about it, Thomas. Yeah, I'll give it some serious thought."

For your consideration:

▶▶ 18-1: Are there any youthful idealists left in our colleges and universities?

▶▶ 18-2: At 35, do you now sometimes catch yourself talking like your parents did? "High ideals don't pay the bills, Panzy." "You think journalism is really the highest calling? There are lots of other ways to contribute to society. One might be to help your parents when they get too old to work. Oh, and do you think journalists don't get taken to court or thrown in jail? Some make up stories. Yours is not exactly the saintly profession you thought you were entering many years ago."

▶▶ 18-3: Your wife was an elementary teacher. She was an idealist, too. You graduated together. She loves her own kids, but she is disgusted by many of the parents of the students she used to teach. Actually, she is also disillusioned with the local school district administration. She quit after you got the publisher's job. She's happy now as a stay-at-home mom. You're not happy. You're wearing a lot of ties these days as publisher. You tell yourself, "If I've got to put on a noose each day, why not put it on in France? Or Italy? And why not have an expense account a bit more enticing than the money you have for pizza when your sales team reaches their ad goals? Why not? And maybe that tie, under the right circumstances, will start to feel a bit more comfortable. French silk? Why not me? Why not now?"

▶▶ 18-4: One more comment to yourself: "Everything involves some kind of marketing and some kind of politics. And spin isn't necessarily a bad word. It's not! Sometimes, we all are advocates. Tell your story. Everyone has a story! Even a rich software firm. More money to give to my church. More money to put away for the kids' college. Money to see that Mom and Dad are taken care of. Those are all noble causes, too. And maybe I'll just go buy a new sports car to help the county economy if I take that job. So many ways to help my family and others. Maybe I need to grow up and face the reality that I'm not a college kid laughing at others' career choices anymore. I come from a minority background. Look at those of my people who are still struggling. I'm OK financially, but why do I believe I'm still struggling? And what, exactly, am I struggling WITH? Oh, to be 21 again!"